PREACHING B

BETHEL SEMINARY WEST
LIBRARY
6116 Arosa Street
San Diego, CA 92115-3902

Abingdon Preacher's Library

PREACHING BIBLICALLY

Exegesis and Interpretation

William D. Thompson

ABINGDON PREACHER'S LIBRARY
William D. Thompson, Editor

Abingdon Press
Nashville

Preaching Biblically: Exegesis and Interpretation

Copyright © 1981 by Abingdon

Third Printing

All rights reserved.
No part of this book may be reproduced in any manner
whatsoever without written permission of the publisher,
except brief quotations embodied in critical articles
or reviews. For information address Abingdon Press,
Nashville, Tennessee.

Library of Congress Cataloging in Publication Data

THOMPSON, WILLIAM D
    Preaching biblically.
    (Abingdon preacher's library)
    Includes bibliographical references and index.
    1. Preaching. 2. Exegesis. I. Title.
    PN44173.B3   251'.03   80-12370

ISBN 0-687-33840-9

Scripture quotations, unless otherwise noted, are from the Revised Standard Version
of the Bible, copyrighted 1946, 1952, © 1971, 1973.

MANUFACTURED BY THE PARTHENON PRESS AT
NASHVILLE, TENNESSEE, UNITED STATES OF AMERICA

CONTENTS

EDITOR'S FOREWORD

Preaching has captured the attention of increasingly large segments of the American public. Lay parish committees seeking pastoral leadership consistently rank preaching as the most desirable pastoral skill. Seminary courses and clergy conferences on preaching attract participants in larger numbers than ever. Millions of viewers watch television preachers every week.

What is *good* preaching? is the question of both those who hear it and those who do it. Hearers answer that question instinctively, tuning in the preacher who meets their needs, whether in the pulpit of the neighborhood church or on a broadcast. Preachers need to answer more intentionally.

Time was that a good thick book on preaching would do it, or a miscellaneous smattering of thin ones. The time now seems ripe for a different kind of resource—a carefully conceived, tightly edited series of books whose scope covers the homiletical spectrum and whose individual volumes reveal the latest and best thinking about each specialty within the field of preaching. The volumes in the Abingdon Preacher's Library enable the preacher to understand preaching in its historical setting; to examine its biblical and theological underpinnings; to explore its spiritual, relational, and liturgical dimensions; and to develop insights into its craftsmanship.

Designed primarily for use in the seminary classroom, this series will also serve the practicing preacher whose background in homiletics is spotty or out-of-date, or whose preaching needs strengthening in some specific area.

> William D. Thompson
> Eastern Baptist Theological Seminary
> Philadelphia, Pennsylvania

I. THE CHALLENGE
OF BIBLICAL PREACHING

The closing decades of the twentieth century cry for preaching that is genuinely *biblical*. The constant threat of nuclear war, the rising number of broken families, and the bewildering dilemmas occasioned by technology combine with a thousand other contemporary problems to demand a word from pulpits that can be heard as an authentic word from the God who reveals himself in the pages of the Scriptures. Preaching that is unbiblical or marginally biblical will not do.

It is not that contemporary preachers fail to take texts from the Scriptures or to quote biblical stories in illustration of their points. Not one of them would boast of being a nonbiblical preacher (well, maybe a few would) or omit the Scripture reading from the service. Their bookshelves groan with various Bible translations: their desks sag with commentaries on the Scriptures: the mail carrier buckles under the load of periodicals offering advice on how to preach biblically. But what they *do* with that embarrassment of riches is the question.

My own tradition advocated "expository preaching" as the epitome of biblical preaching. In their classes and their books my seminary professors told us that expository preaching involved preaching on long texts, while textual preaching utilized short texts. My predecessor in the chair I now occupy in a different seminary taught a generation of students that when both main points and subpoints of the sermon were taken directly from the biblical material, it was an expository sermon: when only the main points came from the Bible, it was textual preaching: and when the points came from one's own brain, the preaching was topical. A great many others define expository preaching as verse-by-verse commentary on a passage of Scripture. Many people believe they are hearing expository preaching when they hear abundant quotations from the Bible, carefully cited as to chapter and verse. What must we conclude? that the terms expository preaching and textual preaching are at least worthless—perhaps dangerous, if they keep us from understanding what *biblical* preaching is.

The key to the matter is whether we define biblical preaching morphologically or substantively. To define it morphologically is to concentrate on its *forms*; does it utilize short or long texts (and how short is short?); does it look at one verse at a time or several (or can the preacher organize the sermon around the *theology* of the text?); where can one legitimately derive the main points (and who remembers the sermon's main points anyway, or cares where the preacher gets them?).

To define the question substantively is to ask more profoundly: how can the preacher make sure that the *substance*, the essence, the core of the sermon is biblical?

One insightful answer is in Donald Miller's book, *The Way to Biblical Preaching*: preaching is "an act wherein the living truth of some portion of Holy Scripture, understood in the light of solid exegetical and historical study and made a living reality to the preacher by the Holy Spirit, comes alive to the hearer as he is confronted by God in Christ through the Holy Spirit in judgment and redemption."[1] Leander Keck puts it another way: "Preaching is biblical when (a) the Bible governs the content of the sermon and when (b) the function of the sermon is analogous to that of the text."[2] These definitions echo the thesis of this book, that *biblical preaching occurs when listeners are enabled to see how their world, like the biblical world, is addressed by the word of God and are enabled to respond to that word.*

One may preach what seems to be a biblical sermon in that the points come from the text, or that every idea is illustrated by some biblical reference, or that one verse after another is "expounded," whatever that means. Treating the biblical material in any of those ways does not insure that it is authentically biblical at all; in other words, that it conveys the message of the Bible. A popular book on biblical preaching provides a model sermon on Colossians 3:18–4:1, for example.[3] The proposition: "The Christian family should live to please the Lord." The outline is:

   I   The wife should submit herself to her own husband. (3:18)
   II   The husband should love his wife. (3:19)
   III The husband (father) should encourage his children. (3:21)
   IV The children should obey their parents. (3:20)
   V   The family servants should obey their employers. (3:22)

One must object strenuously to this maltreatment of the Bible (quite apart from the anachronism of the reference in the late twentieth century to family servants). It is straight, unrelieved, finger-pointing moralism, devoid of any sense of the creative or redemptive purposes of God in Christ or of the power of the Spirit. It is unrelated to the Christian community at Colossae, the Pauline theology which undergirds it, or the Greek social-cultural setting, which might explain why it jars us and makes us look freshly at how God wants to impact contemporary family life. This kind of proof-texting approach to preaching may actually alienate from the Bible those contemporary men and women whose distancing from both the world-view and the theology of the Bible is already too great. It is not at all that some of the things said in such a sermon may not be true or helpful; it is simply not biblical preaching.

Preaching is biblical when it moves a congregation back through history to the east bank of Jordan, for example, to feel despair at the untimely death of Moses, and to wonder if this Yahweh who led us out of Egypt and through the desert even *knows* how desperate is our pilgrimage through the streets of Seattle or Pottstown. It is biblical preaching when we hear him speaking through the centuries to *us:* "Be strong and of good courage . . . for the Lord your God is with you wherever you go" (Josh. 1:9).

Beyond the meaning of the term "biblical preaching" is the corollary question Who cares whether preaching is biblical? Is the attempt to define biblical preaching so much nit-picking? What difference does it make that you or anyone else engage in authentic biblical preaching?

The theological and ecclesiastical communities care deeply, whether gathered on a campus or scattered among the parishes and chaplaincies of the nation. Every seminary dean and judicatory executive knows the letters from angry or perplexed constituents—

lay and clerical—who wonder when the seminary, bishop, executive presbyter, or whoever, will send them a *real preacher* who will make the Bible come alive for them Sunday after Sunday. While theological seminaries have made some strides in the last decade or so in preparing biblical preachers, the hiatus between the preaching lab and the rest of the seminary still calls for a fresh word to integrate preaching with the other tasks of the theological community, both theoretical and practical, and especially with the courses in Scripture.[4]

Certainly the congregation cares that the preaching it hears be biblical. For one thing, its members want and need to be constantly hearing the good news that God was in Christ, reconciling *their* world to himself. To church every Sunday come parents of troubled teen-agers, adults whose singleness is a crushing load, young people suffocating in a depersonalizing high school, grandparents forgotten and unappreciated, children eager for approval. For a time they can endure sermons of good advice, autobiographical revelations, discussions of interesting theological topics, commentaries on the social issues of the day, even explanations of biblical texts. But it was not with such preaching that the church was built, and it is not through such preaching that it will be saved. It is only when they can sense the presence among them of the God of Abraham, Isaac, and Jacob, and the Father of our Lord Jesus Christ that they can become part of the saving tradition, the family of God, the community of the redeemed. However sophisticated their walk down Main Street, it is only when they walk with Christ along the shores of Galilee that they are going anywhere important. However skillful at making choices, they need to stand with Elijah on Carmel and be called upon to choose between Baal and Yahweh. The preacher who makes this happen for a congregation is preaching biblically.

To preach biblically, preachers have always needed to know how to understand and interpret the Bible. The number of books, articles, theses, and audio cassettes that attempt to meet this need is staggering. What has been missing is the single volume in which principles and techniques of biblical exegesis and of biblical interpretation are brought together specifically for the preacher with a view to incorporating the outcome of that study in a sermon.

The purpose of this book is to provide just that help. The procedure is to provide a brief definition of biblical preaching, the subject of this first chapter; to lay out the fundamental tasks of biblical exegesis; to set forth some basic principles of interpretation; and to provide a methodology that is simple enough to enable the construction of an authentically biblical sermon. The book then concludes with the exploration of a biblical text illustrating the procedures, principles, and techniques of the book's theoretical material, and some guidelines for interpreting and preaching from a variety of biblical literature.

II. THE TASK OF EXEGESIS

"Exegesis" is a formidable word. Persons who have not seen it before knit their brows at it; beginning seminary students have heard that it means long hours with unfamiliar books and a long paper to turn in; experienced pastors forget how many steps there are in it.

"Exegesis" is a transliterated Greek word: interestingly, it never appears in the New Testament. The verb form *exegeomai* appears several times and means to tell or to recount. The basic, root meaning is to bring out the meaning of something. Another Greek word, *hermeneia*, becomes the English word hermeneutics, from Hermes, the messenger of the gods. It denotes the process of understanding or interpreting the divine message.

Biblical scholars do not agree on the semantic range of these words, *exegesis* and *hermeneutics*. Granted that the preacher's task is to find meaning for today in the ancient texts, what is the process called? James Sanders calls it a *hermeneutical* process. "The task of biblical hermeneutics today is to seek a mid-point between the *hermeneutical* task of the historical-critical method which seeks original biblical meanings and the *hermeneutical* task of spanning the gap between those recovered meanings and modern cultural systems of meaning. And that task is called canonical *hermeneutics*"[1] (italics added). James Smart, on the other hand, defines the task as *exegesis* . . . a dialogue between the Then and the Now in which the student must be trained if he is not to find himself as a preacher with the biblical text too distant from him for him to hear what it is saying *now*."[2] (italics added).

Perhaps the best clue to the difference between exegesis and hermeneutics is the choice of subtopics which tend to appear in articles and books dealing with these major processes. Writers on exegesis seem to deal largely with questions clustering around a concern for what a biblical writer meant and how that meaning was discerned by those who first read it. They also have a concern for the

PLOT → part of the story
→ something happens
→ conflict

preliterate expressions that found their way into written form—the stories, riddles, songs, liturgies, and other rhetorical forms which were part of the oral tradition of Israel and the early church. The exegetes seem to be the historians, the philologists, the literary critics.

People who write under the rubric of hermeneutics, on the other hand, seem more interested in the meaning of that biblical material for today. They concern themselves with the cultural differences between the ancient and the twentieth-century worlds. They debate about whether we interpret the Bible or the Bible interprets us. They urge us to read the Bible in order to see ourselves in it. Indeed, the question of the person, group, or idea with which the church or believer of today is to identify is one of the most burning hermeneutical issues of the day.

Those who wish to differentiate exegesis from hermeneutics historically or philologically will never do it to the satisfaction of all. About all that is really clear is that the preacher must deal with the meaning-then in order to get the meaning-now. Or is it the other way around, as James Smart suggests? He writes of the distinction "between the meaning then and the meaning now as a treacherous one. The scholar . . . has no access to the original meaning unless the text has some meaning for him now."[3] Certainly he is right. That ability to discuss meaning in both worlds simultaneously, using the insight of the intervening centuries of biblical interpretation, is the goal of every biblical preacher. Most of us, however, do not bring to the task either the years of scholarship or the intellectual equipment of a Smart or a Sanders, a Bultmann or a Barth. We begin at the beginning, working step by step, trying first to understand what happened back there on Mount Sinai or at the potter's house or in Gethsemane. We shall somewhat arbitrarily call that exegesis. Then, remembering that those ancient events were the means by which God spoke to the church freshly in each age, we ask what it is he wants to say to his people today—and through his people to an unbelieving world. We shall call that task hermeneutics or interpretation. And we shall do the best we can with the inevitable overlapping of data.

Prophetic

This chapter takes on the exegetical task, the attempt to discover what the ancient text was all about. Through a series of ordered steps of exegesis, we shall try to determine what happened and why. We want to know how the first readers understood the biblical material. Chapter 3 will deal with the hermeneutical process.

APPROACH TO BIBLICAL EXEGESIS

What kind of book is the Bible? The answer to that question determines our approach to the exegetical task. If it is a rule-book which performs for our lives the function of the final "answer pages" of a fourth-grade mathematics text, we read it in one way. If it is magnificent, inspirational, ancient literature, we read it in another. If it is a book of mysterious signs and symbols about the future waiting to be decoded, we read it in another way still. If it is the inerrant, verbally inspired Word of God, we come at it shaped by that belief.

Perhaps we expect to find ready-made theology in the Bible, or biographical accounts of people whose lives ought to be examples for us. Perhaps we expect the reading of the Bible to awaken our sensitivities to the divine impulses God has placed in the world. Perhaps we shall be satisfied if the Bible is a magnificent literary experience that leads us as no other book into deep understanding of life. Perhaps we think that we shall find in the Bible clear answers to the morally ambiguous questions posed by modern technology—the definition of life as measured by brain waves or the risk of building nuclear power plants. Expect more or less of the Bible than it really is, and the enterprise of exegesis is in trouble.

The Bible defies accurate definition, absolutely unique book that it is. But one must try—to give exegetical study focus and direction, and to avoid false expectations.

At its most basic level, the Bible contains "expressions of belief, value, rituals and world views of particular persons in communities of faith."[4] Beyond that, it is a rich resource of information about the God Yahweh whose people Israel prepared the way for the coming of the Promised One, Jesus Christ. The story of that fulfilled hope is told with a remarkable singleness of purpose and outlook, providing a fundamental unity against which one can place and judge the diverse units of Scripture. The Bible has been and continues to be a source of strength, comfort, and challenge to individual readers, and the conscience of every society whose moral standards are held up to its light.

Supremely, we can expect to find in the Bible the Word of God. It is the story—no, the very action of God revealing himself to his created universe. He speaks, and the world and all its creatures come into being. He unaccountably chooses an obscure nation from Palestine through which to reveal himself and his purposes for every nation under heaven. He strikes down the power of Pharaoh and becomes a pillar of fire to guide his people through the wilderness. By his Spirit, he impregnates a young maiden of his choosing to give birth to his Son, and by his power raises him from the dead. He sends a ragtag group into a corrupt world to turn it upside down. He shares with his people the vision of a new heaven and a new earth over which he will reign in total justice in the eons to come.

Actually, the Bible is not a book at all, but a library of books written over a period of more than a thousand years, bound together to form the primary document out of which the beliefs and practices of the Christian community grow. In the Scriptures God reveals his justice, his love, and his gracious plan for the redemption of his people. The exegetical task is to discover what he *said* about himself and his will so that we may know what he *is saying* about himself and is calling his people to be.

What precisely are we looking for in exegeting that ancient book? One object of our search is our own identity. If it is true that our identity is defined by our history and in our memberships, we shall find them both in the Scriptures. Our history is in Eden where God formed us and breathed life into us; in Egypt from whose bondage he freed us; in Jerusalem at the empty tomb where we come alive with hope. Our membership is in the family of God gathered on Mount Carmel to confront the priests of Baal and in the upper room to sorrow at the deepest loss we shall ever experience. The Scriptures reveal our identity at a profoundly deep level.

The other object of our search is our future; we need some sense of direction as to what God may do and what we should do. If the Bible is anything more to us than a historical curiosity or a literary gem, we turn to it and preach from it because we have the rest of the day to live, or are wondering whether as Christians we should join a march for a non-nuclear world or will soon be eating bread and drinking wine or are trying to cope with the pain and anxiety of family living.

It would be nice to think that we approach biblical exegesis with our minds perfectly open to such information and insights as arise out of careful, objective scholarship. To do that sounds like a great idea, except that it is impossible. If nothing else, our Western culture has been profoundly influenced by the Bible in ways we can never measure. Beyond that is the Bible teaching we have received at our mother's knee, in a catechism class, drinking coffee with the college chaplain, or wherever. We cannot be totally objective students of biblical material.

We can certainly recognize the presuppositions we bring to our task and affirm that they may well be, for the most part, pretty healthy. To say the least, our presuppositions are positive and hopeful. Unless one is reading the Bible solely to find fault, one comes to it ready for new information, new insight, new techniques, new hope for a clear hearing of the word of God for life and ministry.

How, then are we to approach the Bible? Viewed both functionally and theologically and reduced to its essence, the Bible fulfills three basic expectations: (1) *it reveals the human situation apart from God; (2) it records the gracious nature and activity of God; (3) it evokes a response from its readers.* These expectations both provide a rationale for exegesis and control its method. The exegete who is preparing to preach a sermon will dig in the Scriptures to discover valid information specifically about the human problem or question revealed in the text, the good news of God's loving intervention, and the outcome of the human-divine encounter. This threefold view of the Scripture is the theoretical foundation not only of our study of exegetical method, but also of interpretive process and homiletical methodology. It will appear again and again, in different forms, to provide the unifying element in the task of preaching biblically.

Perhaps the most fundamental element in our approach to the Bible is that it can speak to us directly and powerfully even without the rather sophisticated theory and intricate methodology developed in this book. It would be the height of arrogance to suggest that God limits his voice to those who are skilled at exegesis or who can apply a set of interpretive principles to a biblical text. Those of us who bear the responsibility of teaching it and preaching it in the Christian community had better learn exegetical, hermeneutical, and homiletical methodology if we are to be faithful to the task of preserving and passing on the tradition. We start, however, where millions of God's people have started throughout the ages—simply with the open book, through which God has chosen to communicate to those who have sought him. Whatever help lies in human systems of thought are his gift, but his more important gift is the clarity with which he speaks to those who seek him.

EXEGETICAL METHOD

Selection of Biblical Material for Preaching

The idea of choosing a text as the basis for a spoken discourse is an ancient one. Both Old Testament and New Testament preachers based their messages on the oral tradition or written scripture, as have preachers ever since. In dealing with the difficult situations and questions faced by hearers, one instinctively turns to the wisdom of the past.

In general, one can assume that the pericopes which form the lectionary are legitimate preaching units. While there has never been universal agreement in the Christian community about either the value of the lectionary or the appropriateness of its readings, it is clearly one of the most carefully prepared, thoughtful documents available to the preacher. Its three-year cycle is arranged to cover the main events in the life of Israel and of Jesus Christ, the major Christian doctrines, and the major festivals and seasons of the church year. A widely used resource, A *Lectionary*, published by the Consultation on Church Union, includes sixty-eight sets of lections arranged in six seasons.[5] Representatives from the denominations involved in COCU, supplemented by observers from other religious groups, have produced a document of tremendous value to the biblical preacher. Many denominations publish ecclesiastically approved lectionaries and encourage or require their use.

At least two warnings are in order, however, for users of lectionaries. One is the theological filter through which they are modified. In the Roman Catholic lectionary, for example, one of the Old Testament readings in Pentecost is Isaiah 45:1, 4-6. Verse 7, clearly part of the literary structure, is omitted apparently because God describes himself as the one who creates darkness and woe. The other is the cultural filter that omits passages which challenge comfortable, Western life-styles. The COCU lectionary, for example, prescribes Leviticus 19:1-2, 15-18 for the seventh Sunday after Epiphany (Cycle A). The passage calls for holiness in general but omits the concrete, disturbing call to justice laid out in verses 9-13.

Many preachers in the free-church tradition choose texts from week to week on the basis of their own interests or the priorities they establish for the congregation's growth. They may set up a preaching schedule for several months ahead, allowing themselves the liberty of changing the pattern as special needs arise. Their interest in following a lectionary is limited to observing the major events of the church year, such as Christmas and Easter, and perhaps one or two civil observances like Mother's Day. Others use the *lectio continuo* method, preaching through a book of the Bible, one verse or one paragraph at a time.

The need of the congregation is yet another determinant of text selection. At one level, the pastor is aware of the ever-present needs of this congregation, not unlike those of any other. People of older years may be lonely, angry, or hurt at being forgotten by their grown children, anxious about their financial future. Teen-agers are still wobbling between childhood and adulthood, many of them in the congregation because they have been forced to come, others experiencing self-insight at an incredibly deep level. Alienation, celebration, identity, and a thousand other realities characterize situations which call for just the right selection of a preaching text. At another level are those immediate and pressing needs each congregation experiences from week to week. A highly respected congregant has died in tragic circumstances; the annual fund-raising campaign is about to begin; a crucial election is to be held in the coming week: the Word must be the right one.

Whether determined by the preacher's agenda or the congregation's, the text must have a literary integrity. Snatches of Scripture or phrases that are cogent, clever or catchy are, by themselves, seldom legitimate texts for preaching. God has revealed himself historically or in discrete literary units, and the very choice of a text needs to reflect the integrity of that revelation. Let the paragraphing in a good, modern translation provide the clue for the text's literary integrity—or the chapter or even the entire book. Actually, no literary unit should be eschewed in the choice of preaching texts. With sufficient courage, one might even preach a sermon on the whole Bible, highlighting personalities or events or ideas. Some fine sermons have been preached on entire biblical books, either introducing the book's main theme, its key text, some of its minor themes, or perhaps its author or main character. More familiar texts are its small units—paragraphs and sentences. Judiciously chosen, one can preach on combinations of texts as, for example, when the sermon attempts to comprehend all three lections for a given Sunday. Elizabeth Achtemeier advocates pairing of Old Testament and New Testament texts.[6] Some writers on preaching have set up various other combinations.[7] A warning to those whose creativity prods experimentation: do not let the cleverness of text selection get in the way of God's word by calling attention to its cleverness.

Text and Translation

The selection of the text carries with it two fundamental questions: (1) are its words the ones that the original writer used, and (2) how accurately is the meaning conveyed in English? The former question involves us in textual analysis; the latter in translation proper.

Textual analysis, sometimes called "lower criticism," is the province of specialists—biblical scholars who are fluent in Greek, Hebrew, Aramaic, and other ancient languages, and who can readily pick their way through the copyists' errors of haplography, homoeoteleuton, and the like.[8] Their work is of tremendous importance, since no one living has ever seen a manuscript actually written by Paul or Isaiah. We have copies of copies, and not one is an exact duplication of the original.

While no major Christian doctrine is threatened by the variations from an early text to a later one, the meaning of many passages depends on the conclusion of textual critics. One of their many tasks, for example, is to determine punctuation, almost entirely missing in ancient manuscripts. Does Paul call Christ "God" in Romans 9:5? The answer depends on whether the verse is in one sentence or two.

Fortunately for preachers, in seminary or in busy parishes, the results of textual analysis are readily available. The definitive book for the New Testament is A Textual Commentary on the Greek New Testament by Bruce M. Metzger.[9] A system of footnotes, quite easy to understand, informs the reader of the variations in the text and the decision of a committee of first-rate scholars as to the viability of the chosen text. For readers of English only, textual variants may be observed through the footnotes in, say, the Revised Standard Version, which provide alternative meanings or indicate "other ancient authorities read, omit, add, etc."

Obviously, the ability to read Greek and Hebrew significantly enhances one's ability to exegete a biblical text. Learning these languages is easier for some than others, but it is well worth the time and energy for everyone who hopes to preach biblically. While there are abundant translations, the reader of an English translation simply cannot enter into the mood, discern the nuances, feel into the rhythms of the original language. Highly skilled exegetes like to prepare their own translations of the text.

Choosing a translation is the task not only of the person unfamiliar with the Greek and Hebrew. The preacher usually has the freedom to choose the translation to be used in the service of worship of which the sermon is a part. It may be a committee translation like the Authorized Version (usually called the King James Version), the Revised Standard Version, the Jerusalem Bible, the American Standard Version, the New International Version, or the New English Bible. Like other committee assignments, the work may reflect accuracy, caution, and a certain lack of verve, or color. Translations by individuals, like that of The New Testament in

Modern English by J. B. Phillips have become quite popular. A run-away bestseller by an individual, Kenneth Taylor, is The Living Bible, a paraphrase rather than a translation. The choice of a translation is an important one and generally involves both personal preference as to literary style and respect for the objectivity or perhaps for the theological bias of a particular translation source.

To the extent that bias enters translation, the process of selecting a translation is a hermeneutical one. In *Liberation Preaching*, for example, the authors note that most translations of Philemon call Paul a servant and Onesimus a slave, even though the Greek word (*doulos*) is the same for both. "Could it not be that, perhaps unconsciously white translators have been reluctant to have Paul call himself anything as low as a slave?"[10] The New International Version, prepared by conservative evangelicals who interpret some of Isaiah messianically, is careful to translate Isaiah 7:14 "The *virgin* will be with child and will give birth to a son," (italics added) defending the Authorized Version's rendering as over against most other translations which translate the Hebrew *almah* as young woman.

The Triadic Method for Exegesis

The question, what did God do? is a historical one. If the Bible were purely a historical book, the exegetical task would be relatively simple. Even knowing, as we do, that history is interpretation of a miniscule portion of what happened at any point in time, we would still be dealing with only one set of canons. The fact is, however, that the Bible is also a piece of literature in a wide variety of forms, and it is a document of the church that sets forth the church's theology. Our approach, to exegesis, then, takes into account God's choice to reveal himself in the history of a people, both Israel and the new Israel, the church (historical); God's choice to communicate this revelation in some literary form (literary); and his choice of the Bible to be the depository for the church's theology (theological). We shall call our method the exegetical triad.

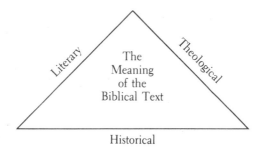

THE EXEGETICAL TRIAD

How did these three dimensions of exegetical method come to be? Until the mid- to late-nineteenth century, students of the Bible believed and formed their theological confessions and practice on what the Bible said with apparent clarity. It was assumed that Old Testament narratives accurately reported "what happened" and sometimes why it happened. Whatever inconsistencies appeared either went unnoticed, were not a serious problem—God being who he is—or would be harmonized in some way at the end of the age. Poetry and figures of speech were generally dealt with for what they were, but really difficult passages could always be connected to Christian doctrine or life through a fanciful allegorization. Newton had laid to rest the notion of a three-storied universe, though that has been one of the more difficult prescientific concepts to put aside from common speech and gesture. But the influence of the Enlightenment, the development of rationalism, and the emergence of the scientific method radically changed the way people read the Bible.

In the late nineteenth century the historical-critical method became the dominant approach to exegesis. It was, for the most part, an honest effort to recreate the actual happenings recorded in the Bible. Because the Bible called for radical changes in human life, both then and apparently now, scholars have studied it critically, calling attention to its verifiable history, but also to its gaps, contradictions, and ambiguities. That dominance has been challenged severely in the last decade or so.

In 1973, Walter Wink shocked the theological community with

the opening assertion in his book *The Bible in Human Transformation* that "historical biblical criticism is bankrupt."[11] Seven years later, James L. Mays, the editor of *Interpretation* underscored the decline of the historical approach to interpretation by writing, "The dominance of historical-critical exegesis seems to be on the wane. A perceptible wariness and weariness at constantly pressing questions about the history of the text's formation and about the history to which the text refers or assumes, as though in combination they were *the* interpretative question, has set in."[12]

Neither Dr. Wink nor Dr. Mays perceives the Bible as a nonhistorical book, nor the Christian faith as built on historical falsehood. Neither do they eschew the methods or results of critical studies insofar as they help readers discover the meaning of the biblical text. The growing disillusionment about historical criticism (with some of the loudest critics from the ranks of the critics themselves!) grows out of the endless nitpicking over minute details of even more minute fragments of the gospel records. Each scholar who works out a hypothesis involving new speculations about the supposedly intricate layering of gospel tradition simply muddies the waters further. Fortunately Old Testament scholarship has enjoyed a fairly benign neglect of this kind of critical study.

The historical questions remain, however, pressing us with the need to know—as far as the evidence will take us—what really happened? That *historical* dimension in the exegetical method becomes the base of the exegetical triad.

In the same issue of *Interpretation* as Dr. Mays' editorial, David J. A. Clines states the case for the *literary* dimension of biblical exegesis by saying that the Bible is written mostly as narrative and poetry and that to read it primarily for history or theology is a mistake.[13] He joins an ever-growing number of scholars who are using the canons of literary criticism for understanding the biblical text. They want to accept and find meaning in a text on its own terms, excluding nothing as invalid—whatever the findings of the historical critic. Secular literary critics have already debated and abandoned what they called "disintegration criticism," the breaking up of literary works into fragments involving misguided efforts to find out which unknown author might possibly have written which phrase in what everybody always thought Shakespeare wrote! The meaning—the value—is in what the material conveys about life, and the beauty with which it does so. The literary dimension, therefore, takes its place as a second dimension of the exegetical triad.

Champion of the *theological* approach to biblical exegesis is James D. Smart. "It was theology which gave birth to history," he writes.[14] That is why, of all the nations, it was Israel that first began to set down a record of the past that was more than a mere chronicle of events. Ancient literature is replete with histories of one civilization or another, stories of both people and their deities. Ideas about truth and justice, about right and wrong, about this world and the world to come are found in all kinds of literature. But the vision of history as a movement of human life toward a goal was born in Israel as a direct consequence of Israel's confrontation with Yahweh. It is the account of that confrontation between Israel and the God of Israel that gives the Bible its unique theological dimension and forces us to discern the biblical text's meaning through the theological dimension of exegetical method.

Where do we begin the task? Ideally, we should ask all the questions at one and the same time. Does the material we are looking at, which obviously occupies a place in history, call our attention to particular events? David's encounters with King Saul are clearly historical narrative, and we can proceed to probe their meaning at that point in history and move on to find meaning for our day. Does not a book like Jonah, on the other hand, tell us that one of the events in Israel's history is that an anonymous writer composed a provocative and entertaining short story to call attention to the provincialism and national arrogance which were hindering the accomplishment of Yahweh's will for his world? Jonah is a piece of literature, but it is also reliable biblical history: that the story was composed, told over and over, preserved as canon and used by the Holy Spirit to reveal *theology*, the nature and will of God for the generations who were to read it, including our own. Whether the events related in that short story are verifiable history is of no greater importance to its meaning than if the elder brother in Jesus' story of the prodigal son really existed. Consistent with the variety of his creation, God chose several literary genres to reveal himself.

We begin, however, with the least complicated of the three dimensions, literary exegesis.

Literary Exegesis

The genre of the biblical book is the first question to be asked in literary exegesis. There is general agreement that Luke-Acts is basically historical material with a strong thread of theological interpretation. The Book of Psalms is poetry, most of it used in the liturgical life of Israel. Philemon is a letter written from one individual to another. Galatians is also a letter, but from an individual to a group of churches in a region. Revelation is apocalyptic material, highly stylized, closely adhering to the rules for a type of writing unique to its time but virtually unknown in today's culture.

Another question to ask is the genre of the particular text. Part of the Book of Daniel is history; part of it is apocalyptic; with which part are we dealing? The Gospel of Luke is essentially historical narrative, but it records Mary's song at the knowledge of the impending birth of Jesus, which is poetry, and which has something of the political tract to it as well (1:46-55). The job of interpretation requires that all three genres be considered. One need not wonder long about the literary nature of any particular biblical unit. A responsible book on the introduction to the Old or New Testament or a good commentary will provide that information quickly.

The discipline which informs the search for genre is *form criticism.* It has reached its greatest sophistication in studies of the Gospels, but is concerned with the fixed forms of discourse everywhere in the Bible. Just as the modern newspaper reader instinctively knows by the form that he or she is reading satire or the report of an accident or a travel column or an editorial or a reader's letter or a bit of gossip, so also can the form critic distinguish among historical narrative, parable, poetry, diatribe, and a host of other fixed forms. [15]

In connection with this step in literary exegesis, one begins to ask questions about the source of the recorded material. If Mary was a poor peasant girl in a society where only men could read and write, can we believe that she personally recorded this very private expression of her feelings? If she did not, who did and under what circumstances? Or was Mary's song actually written by someone at a later time? It was quite common in the ancient Near East for a writer to ascribe to a highly respected person words which he or she might well have employed. Would the material be any less true or useful because it came in a roundabout manner such as this? More often, however, the meaning will be clearer when we *do* know where the materials come from.

The question as to where Mary's words came from is raised by persons working in the discipline of *source criticism.* New Testament scholars have developed a sophisticated set of procedures for trying to determine how one gospel writer drew on the writings of earlier writers. The procedure, however, is fundamentally the same for all biblical study. Unless a book was clearly written by one person, someone had to put together two or more sources for the final version. Source criticism investigates those sources.

The structure of the text or the larger literary unity in which the text is set—usually the entire book—is the second question. Asking about the genre of the text may already have triggered this question. Like haiku poetry with its three lines, or a play which sets up and complicates a conflict and then moves to its resolution, a biblical book always has a literary structure. The book of Romans, for example, is in three quite uneven parts: the first eleven chapters, roughly, deal with theological and philosophical matters, the last four with practical and ethical matters. Sandwiched between the two is the middle section of only four verses (11:33-36) that are doxological. They seem to be placing the heavy theology in context, saying that it is time for the theologizing to stop and that perhaps it has not taken us very far anyway—"Who knows the mind of the Lord?" What follows is also thereby placed in context, the practical advice to the church concerning its behavior and ministry, and the greetings to this one and that. The very structure of the book gives meaning both to the tiny section which is its fulcrum and to the larger units that are related to each other by a passage which may be saying that the praise of God proceeds from theologizing and precedes ministering.

What we have just done is one kind of literary analysis, but looking at structure is also done by the people who do *redaction criticism.* That discipline investigates the structure of biblical books with an eye to how an author's or editor's theological position helps determine why a book looks the way it does. Their concern is with the ways in which the smaller biblical units come together into books through editing or "redacting." A psalm or an epistle may have been recorded by one person in one sitting; the Deuteronomistic history (Deuteronomy through II Kings) and the Synoptics were not. They were carefully edited under the inspiration of the Holy Spirit from a variety of sources to provide a theologically coherent account that was important for the believing community's growth.

Like textual analysis and source criticism, redaction criticism is a skill for highly trained scholars. It is a fairly recent discipline whose ground rules and techniques are not widely agreed upon. That does not mean, however, that the working pastor who is preparing next Sunday's sermon is excused from thinking about the structure of the scriptural material. In the understanding of the theological rationale for the book's construction is to be found a wealth of meaning.

Literary exegesis also asks questions about the very language of the text. It investigates the grammar used by the writer—the declensions of nouns and conjugations of verbs; and the syntax, the ways words are put together in phrases, clauses, and sentences. It makes judgments about style—the distinctive, individual language traits which characterize an author, or even an editor. Stylistic analysis reached some sort of peak—of sophistication or strangeness—in Rudolph Bultmann's work on the Gospel of John. Operating both as redaction critic and stylistic analyst, Bultmann claimed to be able to identify three distinct layers in the Fourth Gospel: the original evangelist himself, sublayers from other major sources, and a final editor. His entire theology of this book is based on this literary analysis.

Historical Exegesis

The task of literary exegesis has already begun to move us into the categories of historical exegesis (*Sitz im Leben* or "setting in life").

We have begun to ask questions that now demand more intentional searching. Who wrote or edited the material as it now stands? For whom was it written and for what purpose? Where was it written, read, and passed on? When was it written? What was going on in the setting which affected its content and style—politically, socially, culturally, religiously?

Even a superficial literary analysis will already have determined whether the material was written by an individual or edited from existing sources. Historical analysis looks more deeply into the five levels of possible authorship possible in ancient literature, including the Bible: (1) actual inscription by a single author; (2) dictation; (3) supplying of ideas to a "secretary-writer"; (4) composition by a disciple under guidance; (5) pseudonymous writing in the tradition for which a person was famous.[16] It is impossible always to know which level one is dealing with, much less who the author was; and it may not matter. The Letter to the Hebrews is certainly the work of one man, but no one has yet persuasively refuted Origen's (A.D. 185–254) opinion that God alone really knows who wrote Hebrews. From internal evidence, however, readers can learn a great deal about the kind of person who wrote it and how those characteristics shaped the book's meaning.

Knowledge of the target audience is indispensable to determining the meaning of the text. Much of the controversy over the differences between the Synoptic Gospels is misplaced if focused on the order of events, the wording of Jesus' sayings, and the like. Many differences are accounted for in terms of the intended audience. Why was the material selected and put together in the way it was? While Matthew was written to communicate the facts of Jesus' life, the audience was clearly that section of the Jewish community which needed insight into the messianic fulfillment that Jesus Christ embodied. Also, the addressees had not yet seen themselves as the new Israel that had replaced the old Israel in the center of God's purpose. Nor had they come to understand the new and higher righteousness embodied in Christ, which exceeded the Jewish law in the radical quality of its demands. While the audience and purpose are not spelled out in the same way as in the Fourth Gospel (John 20:30, 31), the very choice of materials reveals the book's intention.

The location can also reveal a great deal about the meaning of a passage. It is not without reason that a well-equipped church school room, as well as a seminary classroom, provides maps of the ancient world, and that every good Bible includes maps. Slide shows and filmstrips enable the student of the Scriptures to visualize the panorama against which the biblical drama unfolded. It is better yet to visit the Holy Land, as countless thousands of Christian travelers have discovered. The task of exegesis takes on a third dimension for those who have approached Tiberias from the waters of Galilee or walked the Via Dolorosa. Certainly, every person seriously interested in exegesis will have a Bible atlas with up-to-date material on recent archaeological discoveries.

If the exegete's task is to discover what happened, he or she must be able to place a given event at a given time whenever possible. The Psalms defy careful dating, for the most part, although some may take on special meaning if seen as confessions and ruminations of David after his disastrous dalliance with Bathsheba and his encounter with Nathan. The date of I Peter is more important. If it was written by Peter himself, perhaps with the help of Sylvanus, persecution by the Roman emperor was imminent, and the entire book takes on one meaning. If it was written anonymously around A.D. 112, after some of the worst persecutions, its meaning is quite different. A dependable commentary is an invaluable tool in sorting out questions like these.

The setting is the final step in historical exegesis. Traditionally exegetes consider the setting in its political, cultural, and religious dimensions. Political power plays an extremely important role in reconstructing biblical history. Understanding Isaiah, chapters 7 through 10, is impossible without knowing the political situation in Judah under Ahaz, in the Northern Kingdom under Pekah, in neighboring Syria, and in Assyria, the superpower that overshadowed all three smaller nations. The New Testament's passion narratives are profoundly affected by the political tensions between the Jews and the Romans.

Culture as a factor in biblical exegesis has enjoyed more attention in the past few decades than perhaps in the entire history of biblical interpretation. As our knowledge of the ancient world has expanded

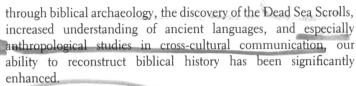

through biblical archaeology, the discovery of the Dead Sea Scrolls, increased understanding of ancient languages, and especially anthropological studies in cross-cultural communication, our ability to reconstruct biblical history has been significantly enhanced.

Studies of material culture focus our attention on items people use in daily living: tools, means of transportation, implements for obtaining and preparing food, weapons, styles of clothing, etc. The story of Jesus' healing of the paralytic let down through the roof (Matt. 9:1-8) makes a great deal more sense, for example, with a knowledge of Palestinian architecture.

Economics, while frequently observable in Scripture only between the lines, was of tremendous importance. Economic instability was a grim fact of life. Famines, the absence of rain, the ravages of war, deportations of entire populations, the threat of defeat and slavery were just a few of the realities in the midst of a people always struggling to survive. Life was short and economic reality harsh for the people of biblical times.

The religious setting is also of great importance to the exegete. Because of the all-pervasiveness of religion in ancient culture, it does not separate neatly from the other factors: material, economic, and social. Specifically and exclusively religious places and practices can be identified, however. For the most part, religious life came to expression in the temple, in synagogues, and in house churches where Christians met to break bread and hear the Word preached. The great feasts and other religious observances of Israel open deep meaning for the Christian exegete. Passover as the religious setting in which Jesus went to his death has profound implications for the passion narratives, for example.

Reconstruction, then, is the object of historical analysis, utilizing all that can be learned about the text's authorship, audience, place, date, and setting. One final element is needed to complete the puzzle: the checking for parallel passages. Many "harmonies of the Gospels," for example, have been published, setting in parallel columns the events of Jesus' life. These are of considerable importance, but they raise certain questions. Many New Testament scholars eschew these efforts, asserting that they violate the integrity of a Gospel writer's work, reducing it, perhaps unintentionally, to a simple chronology, and fuzzing his theology. At the same time, the multiplicity of accounts of a given situation is most enriching, and the events of Jesus' ministry especially so. The conquest of Canaan is recorded both in Judges 1 and 2 and in the first twelve chapters of Joshua. The stories obviously do not jibe, so how can one reconstruct them? The New Testament gives us four accounts of the trial of Jesus. What to do with them? We may attempt to synthesize them, become upset because they contradict each other, or conclude that we still do not know what happened since none of the writers was there anyway.

What we may be faced with, then, is distinguishing between the attempt to reconstruct what probably happened and to exegete the *reports* of what happened. Accurate reconstruction is possible in many texts, but where it is not, the honest exegesis of just what is there—questions, varying data, or whatever—may provide even richer resources for understanding. Keck and Tucker conclude that "historical-critical exegesis has destroyed the impact of old arguments against the Bible because there were 'contradictions' in it. Diversity and tension are to be expected."[17]

Theological Exegesis

Biblical writers are, to varying degrees, also theologians. Not one is what we would call a systematic theologian, but their object in writing is to reveal the nature and activity of God. The exegete's job of theological analysis (*Sitz im Glauben*, the "faith situation") is to discover what phrases of theology are being addressed and what is being said about them. One of many useful theological configurations for exegetes is in the contents of Gabriel Fackre's book, *The Christian Story*: (1) Prologue: God; (2) Creation; (3) Fall; (4) Covenant; (5) Jesus Christ: Person and Work; (6) Church: Nature and Mission; (7) Salvation; (8) Consummation; (9) Epilogue: God.[18] God is clearly the beginning and the end of the theological process; he determines and is described by the categories he alone can embrace. A rough sort of systematic theological analysis would place a text under one of these rubrics.

Take just three of these categories, for example, to see how one can discern the theological motif in a biblical passage. In the various episodes of the Exodus stories, for example, the theological theme of *salvation* dominates the material. The release by Pharaoh, the crossing of the Reed Sea, the provision of manna—all are acts by Yahweh to save his people. Another salvation theme is taken up in the New Testament by Paul whose theological masterpiece is Romans 5:6-11, "While we were yet sinners Christ died for us." In Colossians 1:15-20, Paul moves to a distinctively *christological* theme, a passage whose centerpiece is 1:17: "He is before all things, and in him all things hold together." The theological theme of I Thessalonians 4:13-18 is *consummation*; it is a detailed explanation of the events at the end of the age as the author saw them unfolding: "For the Lord himself will descend from heaven with a cry of command."

Another approach to theological analysis, suggested by Victor Paul Furnish, might be called *situational.* He wants the exegete to see the implicit relationships among the text's various ideas and convictions as related to the life situation which produced that text. How did the earliest Christians, for example, receive the tradition into the various situations where they lived and worked? In what sense and to what extent did the theology of a particular author shape the ongoing life of the church?[19]

The Epistle to the Hebrews, for example, is strongly christological but is set in an apocalyptic framework (to take only the dominant two of the many theological motifs of the book). To the author of the book, the primary theme is that Christ had offered the true and complete sacrifice and is now ministering as the high priest in the heavenly holy of holies. But the framework of that assertion is a view of history as the unfolding, dynamic purpose of God with the corollary belief that God is about to bring the present age to an end and inaugurate a new age. What is important in a theological exegesis is that the persons addressed were Jewish Christians under persecution who may have been in danger of abandoning their Christian commitment. Part of their movement away from Christ was their inability, to that point, of fully understanding the all-sufficiency of Christ as authentic Messiah; part was their inability

Prophetic look [handwritten annotation]

to hold fast in the life-threatening situation in which they had to reevaluate their religious experience. In the juncture of these two dynamic forces, the Word of God could be made clear.

Yet another approach to theological analysis is the historical understanding of the text in the continuing life of the community of faith. Part of the mystery of the Word is that it keeps breaking loose into new meanings for each generation. Brevard Childs, both in his brilliant commentary on the book of Exodus and his *Introduction to the Old Testament as Scripture*[20] posits the meaning of each text in the canon as a whole, that is, by its final context. The theological intention of its writer, therefore, may be less important than its meaning in later generations. The logical extension of that principle leads to the study of the text's meaning beyond the canonical period, into the interpretations by the church throughout the centuries, and, indeed, down to the interpretations of our own day.

Resources

ch. hist → Cath. TRAD → Protec. [handwritten annotation]

The role of scholarship has permeated the description of exegetical method. While the use of the English text alone can produce significant information on what happened and why, the most accurate and useful insights depend on the kind of help offered by the community of scholars who, combined, have spent thousands of lifetimes checking out ancient manuscripts, comparing parallel Gospel accounts, delving deeply into the meaning of Syro-Phoenician words, becoming familiar with the daily life of preexilic Israel, investigating the fixed literary structures of Hebrew poetry, and so on.[21]

The first and most important resource is an accurate and sensitive English translation of the Bible. Even the most skilled reader of the original languages turns now and again to a good English translation to see what another skilled individual or a prestigious committee has done with a particularly perplexing text. Today's exegete experiences an embarrassment of riches in Bible translations. The exegete will want to have as many of the translations as can be purchased.

The second resource lies on the very pages of many of those translations: the introductory pages of each book often contain the kind of analytical information called for in this chapter. While seldom providing much depth, the insights may be valuable enough in themselves to undergird the next steps of interpretation and preaching. They may also serve to open questions that can be pursued in more specialized resources.

Two good concordances constitute the third resource: one exhaustive and the other topical. The exhaustive concordance lists in one place every location in the Bible at which a particular *word* is used. The topical concordance attempts to list the locations in the Bible at which the same *idea* is used; i.e., it deals in synonyms. In the search for the idea of obedience, for example, one may find four or five times as many texts in a topical concordance as in an exhaustive one. It refers the exegete to verses such as the commandment in Deuteronomy 5:32, which clearly calls for obedience but does not use the word, and Matthew 11:26 in which Jesus is obeying the Father.

Books of word studies are also a valuable resource. While the richest and most extensive works cover the Greek of the New Testament and the Septuagint, many valuable volumes are also available to provide insight into Old Testament Hebrew. The exegete can choose from a wide range of books, exhaustive, multivolume works or relatively simple books designed for lay teachers of adult Bible classes.

The fifth category of exegetical resources is the commentary, the selection and use of which requires careful thought. The most useful commentary is one which confines itself to the kinds of analyses set forth in this chapter; it is not properly a source of sermon ideas or illustrations. The interpretive process has to spring from the preacher's application of hermeneutical principles carried out in the dynamics of a believing community's life. One should choose a fairly recent commentary that draws upon the latest and best research and thinking in linguistics, archaeology, biblical theology, literary criticism, and ancient history. It should be eminently fair, setting forth the various positions on controversial questions. It should also point the reader to books, articles, and monographs which further illuminate the matter at hand.

Dictionaries and encyclopedias are yet another category of resource material. A Bible dictionary is generally a one-volume work that provides fairly brief definitions and explanations of the major people, places, and concepts of the Bible. An encyclopedia is a multivolume work, performing much the same function, but in a far more comprehensive manner. The range of choice is considerably more limited than in the category of commentary.

Similarly limited in choice, but no less important for the exegete's library, is the Bible atlas. While some atlases contain only maps, it is far better to secure one whose extensive supply of maps function, not only on their own, but represent illustrations of responsible accompanying text on the geographical history of the Holy Land and the ancient world.

There are a great many other helpful books on the market that are helpful to the student of the Bible, each succeeding publishers' list offering new and creative combinations of useful reference materials. The Bible handbooks, interlinear translations, parallel Bibles, studies of daily life in ancient times, materials on biblical archaeology, translation handbooks, lexical aids, and specialized monographs can all contribute to the exegetical task in significant ways. The wise exegete will regularly read advertisements, articles, and reviews on periodicals for ministers to keep abreast of the emerging resources.

For the preacher who is able to read the original biblical languages three final categories present themselves: lexicons, concordances of Greek and Hebrew, and grammars. The lexicon, whether of Greek or Hebrew, deals with the meaning of words and their etymology (roots). The most useful consists of two parts: one beginning with the biblical word translated into English with all the shades of meaning and uses, the other beginning with the English word which refers to the term in Greek or Hebrew. The concordance of Greek or Hebrew functions exactly like the concordance to the English Bible except that the Greek or Hebrew words control the arrangement of material. Grammars are more complex than either. They analyze sounds (phonology), forms (morphology), and relationships (syntax).

The study of *sounds* is for the most part of interest only to the specialist. In some cases, however, the sound of a word is an important clue to its meaning, as, for example, in Isaiah 5:7 whose puzzling meaning is made clearer by knowing that the English words simply cannot adequately translate "he looked for "justice" [*mišhpat*], but behold "bloodshed" [*mišpah*]; for "righteousness" [*sĕdākāh*], but behold "a cry" [*se͑āqāh*]. The study of *forms* releases rich insights of meaning. Tense, mood, voice, person, and number determine how a verb is to be understood. Case opens the meaning of nouns: eight of them in Greek, none as such in Hebrew. *Syntax* is the study of how words, phrases, and clauses are related to each other. The study of syntax enables us to distinguish parallel ideas, or to distinguish in a given sentence which element may help to shape or determine an idea and which is shaped by it. The purpose of a grammar is to lead the exegete through the maze of possibilities to the most accurate understanding of the text.

Finding out what happened and why and what it may have meant to its original and to succeeding audiences is the difficult, sometimes frustrating, always exciting task of exegesis. The resources are plentiful and the task rewarding beyond measure for the one who is seeking the reality of God in a world that needs him desperately. Our attention now turns to our world and the task of interpreting for its people the Word which transcends time and space.

III. THE PROCESS
OF INTERPRETATION

The exegetical task has been to attempt the reconstruction of the meaning of the biblical text to give us some clues as to how it might have been understood by the original reader and subsequent generations; the hermeneutical task is to interpret that text for our contemporaries: "so to interpret the Scriptures that the past becomes alive and illumines our present with new possibilities for personal and social transformation," as Walter Wink puts it.[1] We call it the process of interpretation.

PRESUPPOSITIONS

Everything we read and experience is affected by our presuppositions. By the time we are old enough to read and understand this book, we have stored a great deal of knowledge, formed a great number of opinions, and have been enriched and hurt by a great many relationships. We can focus upon only a tiny fraction of the traditions that have helped to shape us: for example, the way we have observed birthdays and anniversaries—and observe them now; the way we have understood and celebrated Holy Communion—in our childhood and now. Our presuppositions comprise a complex of attitudes, emotions, beliefs, myths, prejudices, ideas, and interests. Bultmann rightly insists that "there cannot be any such thing as presuppositionless exegesis."[2]

We bring those presuppositions to the interpretation of a biblical text; we cannot avoid them if we want to. Our minds do not constitute a *tabula rasa* on which will be written the pure Word of God, directly from a text. Assuming an openness to the inbreaking of the Word through the Holy Spirit, there must also be some basis for theological understandings about God, humanity, the nature of Scripture, and the role of Christian experience.

If, as we have said, the arena of our preaching is the future, then we can preach only if God is changeless, eternal, and always good—the same in the future as he was in the past. We shall tell worshipers that God will forgive their sins upon repentance; that in the valley of the shadow of death they will be able to experience the presence of the Good Shepherd; that in eternity God will say to those who mouthed, "Lord, Lord," but acted unjustly, "I never knew you; depart from me" (Matt. 7:21-23). If God were capricious, we could not preach those messages, or any others for that matter. The message of the Christian preacher is "Jesus Christ, the same yesterday, today, forever" (Heb. 13:8).

It is not only that pragmatic line of reasoning that makes our first presupposition the eternality of God, but the witness of the mainstream of Christian theology throughout the centuries. Most Catholic, Protestant, and Orthodox theologians join in affirming God as predictably omnipotent, eternal, omniscient, and true. In our day, Wolfhart Pannenberg has built his view of reality as a unity that is grounded in the biblical affirmation of the oneness or unity of God. To him, theology is a theology of world history with the historical process as a continuum connecting past and present.[3] That predictability—that oneness of God in the dimension of time—is fundamental to the connection; it also enables us to talk coherently about God. Jurgen Moltmann puts it yet another way when he speaks of God's future continually invading the human present.[4]

What we expect of God is that he will function among us as he always has, creatively and redemptively. Because we affirm the continuation of his *creative purposes* in the world, we can, for example, speak of money as God's gift to us, a part of his creation, of which he makes us stewards. As Christians, we join the effort to preserve the creative work of God by opposing the wanton denuding of forests, the abuse of nuclear power, the waste of human energy in urban centers of unemployment. Because we acknowledge and celebrate the *redemptive work* of Jesus Christ, we offer the possibility of new life in him—rich, abundant, eternal. We give thanks whenever and wherever reconciliation takes place—in the offices of labor mediators, in the signing of peace treaties between nations, in the counseling office where Christian foundations are laid for the renewal of family life, and, supremely, at the altar rail or its equivalent where persons find new life in Christ. To the guilt-ridden we say that there is forgiveness in him; to the lonely we announce the presence of a constant friend; to the oppressed we proclaim liberty.

While God may surface in unexpected places and at times we cannot predict and in ways we would never have guessed possible, his nature and activity are constant and eternal and good. That is the first presupposition on which we build.

The second presupposition is the continuity of human nature and experience. If there were a radical discontinuity between us and the humanity of ancient Israel or of the New Testament era, it would be impossible to preach and unnecessary to interpret the Scriptures. Suppose that a perfect, sinless Jesus-like figure appeared every few decades in the biblical narrative. Unthinkable! you say. Precisely so. So consistent in the Scriptures is the fallibility of human beings that we cannot even get our minds around that supposition. The uniqueness of Jesus Christ, the God-man, would be destroyed—indeed, the whole story of redemption carried from Genesis to Revelation would become ludicrous. We should be thrown on the search for who that perfect being might be the next time (could it be me?) rather than to look honestly at the ways we have fallen short of the glory of God and stand in need of his love and forgiveness. Leander Keck puts it this way: "Certain perversions of life and of Christian faith are perennial, paradigmatic; indeed one may even call them archetypal."[5] While God created us in his own image, and therefore good, we have "all sinned and fallen short of the glory of God" (Rom. 3:23). We shall never understand the meaning of the Scriptures or be able to preach from them apart from that dismal but accurate truth.

That commonness of understanding links not only hearers of biblical times with hearers in our churches, but it underlies the entire hermeneutical process. To Ernst Fuchs a central motif of the "new hermeneutic" is the assertion that "all understanding is grounded in Einverstandnis (variously translated "mutual understanding," "agreement," or "empathy")."[6] Members of a close-knit family share a common world of values and experiences, and therefore, a common language. Jesus' parables, based on common experiences, demonstrated that presupposition with clarity and power.

The unity and authority of the biblical revelation is the third presupposition. Of all the religious books and collections of writings ever written, we base our preaching on the Holy Bible, the Christian Scriptures, the Old and New Testaments. Why? One reason is that it is the giver of our tradition. We and our Jewish neighbors have always been people of the Book. From the inscription of the Ten Commandments on stone to the apocalyptic writings of John at Patmos, the Word of God has occurred in written form as well as by the voice of God and the inner witness of the Spirit. Another reason is that we who have searched the Scriptures have found in them the words of eternal life; our experience with the Bible is that it authenticates itself; it hangs together—in all its diversity—and cements our faith in it as the place to go for information about God and guidance for living.

That word "revelation" is a most important one in understanding the role of the Bible in preaching. Revelation (*apocalyptein*) literally means an unveiling so as to disclose something that was formerly hidden. Paul spoke of "the revelation of the mystery which was kept secret for long ages but is now disclosed" (Rom. 16:25). That mystery is the will and purpose of God. In one sense, revelation is information about God disclosed in the pages of the Bible. In another, it is not so much information about God that is revealed but God himself, come in the person of his son Jesus Christ. Kittel defines revelation as "the *action* of Yahweh, an unveiling of His essential hiddenness, His offering of Himself in fellowship."[7] Revelation then, may be understood as proposition, but only secondarily; revelation is primarily Person.

The word "authority" (*exousia*) needs to be understood also. While revelation denotes the *content* of God's message in the Bible, authority denotes its *value*, its power, its influence. In an age when authority is not a popular concept, preaching from an authoritative Bible is problematic, to say the least. Authoritative persons and concepts are not heeded as we like to think they once were—parents, law enforcement officers, sexual taboos, standards of workmanship.

Nevertheless, the choice of a biblical text for preaching carries with it, if only implicitly, the force of authority, of high value. The Bible's authority may or may not have to be defended in any given situation, but it must undergird the preaching enterprise.

Another word, "inspiration" (*theopneustos*), is the *process* of transmission and preservation of God's self-revelation. It is generally thought of as the work of the Holy Spirit and is most clearly set forth in II Timothy 3:16 "All scripture is inspired by God and profitable for teaching, for reproof, for correction, and for training in righteousness." The method and significance of that inspiration continues to be a matter for debate; and there is no shortage of debaters! The fact that God's Spirit brought the Scriptures into being and that they are authoritative for faith and life will have to suffice for us now.

Value, however, cannot be understood only in objective terms of the inherent or intrinsic worth of a word offered; it must also be understood in subjective terms, of a word received. It does not matter that the church, the preacher, or God himself considers the biblical revelation to be authoritative; it has no value unless the person hearing that word affirms its value. The parent who says authoritatively that the family car will not leave the premises may find keys, car, and teen-ager gone. Where is the authority?

If one wishes to count churchly noses, it is the believers in biblical authority who are today crowding the churches. Billy Graham's repeated, "The Bible says . . ." both reflects his own belief in the Bible's authority and is a device to convince the audience or to reinforce its belief in the value of the Scriptures. The hunger for an authoritative word in our day is a deep one. The issue of which biblical affirmations have authority and in what ways they are authoritative will be discussed later. The interpretive enterprise proceeds, however, on the general presupposition that the Bible contains God's authoritative word for us.

The final presupposition with which we approach the process of interpretation is the necessity of Christian experience. Certainly anyone can derive value from reading the Bible. Much of it—perhaps most of it—is understandable on its own terms. The historical narratives, the poetry, the character studies, all of them have tremendous value for any reader. The interpreter—preacher or teacher—cannot function, however, without personally participating in the community of faith which produced, preserved, and now lives by the power of the Scriptures. Nor can the interpreter who belongs to that community do so apart from a personal experience of redemption in Jesus Christ.

In his First Letter to the Corinthians, Paul offered the clearest and most powerful rationale for this assertion in his discourse on the interpretation of spiritual truths (I Cor. 2:6-16). It is only the Spirit of God, he says, that can comprehend the thoughts of God, and it is precisely that Spirit which Christians have received in Jesus Christ. It follows, then, that "we impart this in words not taught by human wisdom but taught by the Spirit" (2:13). Conversely, "the unspiritual [natural] man does not receive the gifts of the Spirit of God, for they are folly to him, and he is not able to understand them because they are spiritually discerned" (2:14).

A preacher may have both exegetical skill and interpretive insight, then, and still be unable in any ultimate way to communicate the Word of God. What of the real-life Elmer Gantrys who travel from one revivalist tent to another or who settle into comfortable parishes as *de facto* atheists and live a lie? There are some of them around! On the other hand, one may point to persons of deep and authentic Christian faith whose exegetical sloppiness and occasional interpretative mishaps seem not to hinder their ministries. No matter. The goal—the ideal—is Christian experience augmented by scholarly skill. The truth confirmed and authenticated by centuries of Christian tradition, if not by the mind of God, is that only the preacher who has experienced the reality of God can even begin to communicate that experience with power and with lasting effect.

If the preacher's Christian experience is the *sine qua non* of biblical preaching, it will be embodied by that preacher in the experiential reality of the first three presuppositions: in (1) one's continuing sense of need for the grace of God, (2) in relationship with that gracious God, and (3) in a familiarity with the record of the peoples' response to God's grace as recorded authoritatively in the Bible. If this threefold apparatus looks like the expectations with which we entered upon the task of exegesis, the similarity is intentional. The application of hermeneutical principles and techniques that follow will be valuable to the extent that they enable the preacher to help elicit response to the God who meets people in their need.

PRINCIPLES

It would be a mistake to offer a set of rules for interpreting the Bible. Using rules, one can be certain that the gin rummy game is being played correctly; using instructions, one can assemble a ten-speed bicycle; following directions, one can bake an edible pound cake. The Bible, however, is an incredibly complex collection of literary forms which alone makes the task difficult, not to speak of the "spiritual" dimension which involves the interpreter in the realm of the ineffable, the mystical.

Although it is an oversimplification, one can say that science proceeds on rules; art on principles. Oil painting has a scientific dimension in that a scientist can describe with accuracy the chemical composition of the oils, the brush, the canvas, and can measure and weigh the objects in the still life—oranges, candle, linen table cover. But the artist and the art critic operate in another realm, the realm of principles—of balance, proportion, texture, color, perspective. Just so in biblical preaching are there both scientific and artistic dimensions. To some extent, though not so clearly as the scientist, the exegete operates with relatively objective procedures in the study of comparative religions, the investigation of syntax, genealogy, and etymology. The interpreter, on the other hand, must work with principles that provide a certain amount of guidance for both artist and critic, but that always leave room for discussion and debate.

Principles are statements which materially affect the way we handle the text and which must be taken into account to arrive at conclusions about the text's meaning. They are not sequential steps to be followed, except insofar as they are generally applied one at a time. Nor are they inviolable rules which either guarantee accurate meanings in their observance or deny those meanings in their omission. What they constitute is a framework, a matrix to provide both a procedure for approaching a biblical text and a critical apparatus for evaluating the adequacy of one's own or another's interpretation. While they are stated positively, they also perform the negative role of warning against false interpretations.

What follows is an attempt to state a coherent and useful set of ten principles for interpreting the Scriptures.

1. Simplicity

The starting point for biblical interpretation is the clear, plain meaning of the passage.

John Calvin said several centuries ago in his commentary on Galatians: "Let us know, then, that the true meaning of Scripture is the natural and obvious meaning; and let us embrace and abide by it resolutely. Let us not only neglect as doubtful, but boldly set aside as deadly corruptions, those pretended expositions which lead us away from the natural meaning."[8] Calvin did not mean that Scripture is always to be taken literally; figures of speech permeate biblical writings. Nor did he advocate inattention to context or careful scholarship. What he did mean is that the interpreter should not bypass the obvious meaning to seek out a "deeper meaning" because the text does not convey truth as he or she sees it or would like to phrase it; we are people who are "under the word."

A great amount of scriptural material—indeed, most of it—is understandable on its own terms. What could be more plain than I John 1:5? "This is the message we have heard from him and proclaim to you, that God is light and in him is no darkness at all"? Is there any doubt about Ezekiel's meaning when he conveyed the Word of the Lord who said: "Son of man, prophesy against the shepherds of Israel, prophesy, and say to them, even to the shepherds, 'Thus says the Lord God: Ho, shepherds of Israel who have been feeding yourselves! Should not shepherds feed the sheep?" (Ezek. 34:2)? Who cannot resonate with Naomi who heard her widowed daughter-in-law say, "Entreat me not to leave you or to return from following you; for where you go I will go, and where you lodge I will lodge; your people shall be my people, and your God my God" (Ruth 1:16)?

The context of Calvin's advice was the widespread practice in his day of allegorizing scriptural texts, which involved making a narrative convey totally different ideas than were intended by the author, usually because the face value of the story carried unacceptable data or meaning. Origen (A.D. 185–254) found in the story of Rebecca's drawing water for Abraham's servant and his cattle the lesson that we must come to the wells of Scripture to meet Christ! (Gen. 24:1-51)

The principle of simplicity is further abused in allowing imagination or wishful thinking to put meaning into a text that is simply not there; it is called *eisegesis*, or "reading into" the text something foreign to it.

Ronald A. Knox's sermon "The Window in the Wall" illustrates eisegesis. The message is presumably based on Song of Solomon 2:9 whose speaker discerns her love "on the other side of this very wall . . . calling to me, 'Rise up and come with me.' " Msgr. Knox sees God who "stands behind 'our wall,' the wall of our corrupt nature, which shuts us off from breathing, as man breathed in the days of his innocency, the airs of heaven; the wall of sense, which cheats us when we try even to imagine eternity; the wall of immortified affection, which shuts us in with creatures and allows them to dominate our desires; the wall of pride, which makes us feel, except when death or tragedy is very close to us, so independent and self-sufficient . . . through that wall, the Incarnation and the Passion of Jesus Christ have made a great window."[9] Eisegesis makes a text mean something it certainly did not mean to earlier readers and is a fundamentally dishonest activity. It also sets a bad example for sermon-listeners who are Bible readers and who need a good example for discerning the plain meaning of the text.

Another way to abuse the principle of simplicity is not to deal honestly with the obviously figurative language or to refuse to take into account the cultural conditioning of particular texts. Simplicity is not simple-mindedness. A sect called the Children of God recruited thousands of young people during the sixties and seventies and appealed to them to leave their homes, even to literally hate their parents on the basis of Jesus' condition for discipleship in Luke 14:26: "If anyone comes to me and does not hate his own father and mother and wife and children and brothers and sisters, yes, and even his own life, he cannot be my disciple." That text is not to be understood "simply"; Jesus was using hyperbole, a common figure of speech using exaggeration for effect. Another example: Paul's instructions to the Corinthian church (I Cor. 11:2-16) give detailed prescriptions for the length of people's hair, all of it related to the prevailing opinions about the inequality of the sexes and the length of hair which were socially acceptable at that time. Some Christians have interpreted the passage simply and normatively. Likewise, his injunction to women to veil their heads while praying determined for centuries the practices of many churches which prescribed hats for women during Sunday worship.

The principle of simplicity—or perspicuity, as it is sometimes called—is not to be understood as meaning that the interpretation of Scripture is simple, that is to be interpreted literally, or that each text has a single meaning; it is to say that much of the time, the meaning of Scripture is powerful and clear without digging or distorting, and that simple common sense is to be exercised in the process of interpretation.

2. Intentionality

God intends the Bible to communicate his creative and redemptive purposes in Jesus Christ.

The principle of intentionality simply says that there is reason to be discovered for every passage in the Bible; a reason for its being there and a reason for our knowing about it. The term itself is borrowed from phenomenology and has emerged into theological language through the "new hermeneutic." Intentionality as a concept means more than the "message" of the text, which might limit itself to a kind of propositional understanding of the faith. It involves a kind of crawling into the mind and spirit of the text to sense the dynamics of what was being written, spoken, or sung.

How is one to discover the intentionality of the text? The answer lies in the skill with which the exegesis has been done. When the preacher has come to understand through historical-literary-theological study of the passage, the message of the author or editor, intentionality begins to emerge. It is the single most fundamental question to be asked of the enterprise—Why is this text there? If it is not asked and satisfactorily answered, no other step, technique, or insight matters.

The simplest and most productive way to get at a text's intentionality is to postulate the opposite, i.e., to view from inside the author's mind the situation in which God impelled him to write, preach, see the vision, sing, or whatever. Some kind of circumstance called that word into being—an unruly church, a gathering for worship, a group trying to sort out law and grace, a slaveowner awaiting the return of a runaway, a wealthy and comfortable nation partying itself into judgment, a tiny band of Christians awaiting the knock on the door by Nero's soldiers. Ask what difference did it make that the word was heard, or what difference would it have made if it *had* been heard and acted upon?

The answer will come out as a theological or an ethical statement or both. To the unruly Corinthian church, to which Paul's first letter went, the word is that they will not communicate their faith in Christ by fighting among themselves, by conforming to the immorality all around them, by misunderstanding Christian liberty, by confusing the proportioning of gifts. They will communicate their faith if they will make love their aim, and, in that love, live in the magnificent expectation of Christ's return. That is something of the intentionality of the book. A shorter pericope within the book will have a different, more specific purpose, but it will be a part of that larger purpose.

One can also come at the task more simply yet by reversing the words of the text. Paul wrote to the Philippians, "But one thing I do, forgetting what lies behind and straining forward to what lies ahead, I quit." No, it is "I press on toward the goal for the prize of the upward call of God in Christ Jesus." (3:13, 14). But to reverse the main idea of the text—or even one of the secondary ideas—is to provoke one's thinking and homiletical creativity. What would the early church have been like if Paul had indeed quit when he remembered what lay behind and reflected that he would meet many of the same problems in the future, or worse?

To say that every passage has a reason does not mean that the reason is immediately apparent: it may take considerable digging to find it. Nor is it to say that, having found a text's meaning, it is

BETHEL SEMINARY WEST
LIBRARY
6116 Arosa Street
San Diego, CA 92115-3902

preachable for a given occasion, or ever. There are exciting, challenging texts that cry out to be preached, and others of less value. At some point in Israel's history, Ezra, chapter 2 was important, but what is the value today, for example, of the list of temple servants in that chapter? The need for that information, either for theology or ethics, simply does not exist in our day. Its original intentionality is of academic interest, but nineteen centuries have removed it from the vital issues of the day. It does not immediately communicate the creative and redemptive purpose of God, and we instinctively bypass it in our search for texts to preach.

Writers in the "new hermeneutic" school express the principle of intentionality solely in terms of the text's addressing us. They are uncomfortable with traditional hermeneutics that investigates the text as the object of knowledge. It is based on the philosophy of Descartes, they say, in which understanding is perceived as knowledge, rather than experience. James Robinson offers the alternative view. In the new hermeneutic, "the flow of the traditional relation between subject and object, in which the subject interrogates the object . . . has been significantly reversed. For now it is the object—which should henceforth be called the subject-matter—that puts the subject in question."[10] Put more popularly, it is the text which interprets us, which illumines our lives, rather than we working to interpret the text.

However one determines the intentionality of the text, the weight is certainly with the new hermeneuts in that God does not intend the Bible to be the object of our attention, a book to be studied for its own sake, but rather intends it to change human lives.

3. Correspondence

The basic interpretative process involves correspondence between the biblical and the contemporary worlds.

A fundamental question in biblical interpretation is How does the word to an ancient people become the word to contemporary people—to us? Given a valid statement of the text's intentionality, derived through exegesis, how can we be sure that there is a valid

"Spirit" of the living Word

linkage between the word God spoke and the word he wants to speak now?

The importance of correspondence as a basic principle of interpretation is suggested by the number of synonyms for the idea. Writers on interpretation describe the relationship as correlation, historical continuity, similarity, identification, transference, parallelism, linkage, analogy, resemblance, paradigm, or comparability. While shades of meaning differ, the basic idea, to use a different figure yet, deals with the journey from the past to the present and with both the pitfalls and the possibilities of that journey.

Elizabeth Achtemeier exemplifies the principle in her handling of Deuteronomy 30:15-20 ("I have set before you life and death . . . therefore choose life"). "How can we enable our people to identify with this Deuteronomy text? . . . We can do so by the method of analogy. We Christians have become members of Israel, and so this is *our* story in Deuteronomy; Israel's total situation there before God is remarkably parallel to our total situation before him. We are both underway. We both have been redeemed out of slavery. We both have not yet entered into our final fulfillment. We both have a response asked of us by God." [11]

The task is described by Leander Keck who writes: "Whereas the hermeneutical task of imparting the biblical meaning is focused on the content of the text, the hermeneutical issue here focuses on the way one correlates the original readers and today's readers. There we reflected on the hermeneutics of the content, here we focus on the hermeneutics of the recipients, then and now. The preacher must identify what today's hearers share with the authors' original readers so that the text confronts them both." [12]

For a great many biblical texts, the journey is not difficult at all. The message conveyed by Joshua to God's people on the brink of Jordan was clear enough, as they prepared for the conquest of Canaan: "Be strong and of good courage; be not frightened, neither be dismayed; for the Lord your God is with you wherever you go" (Josh. 1:9). The fact that the conquest of Canaan had limited success does not alter the promise or the reality of the presence of God in the midst of his people. In this case the journey from Jordan to Peoria is not far or difficult. The church under new and untried leadership can hear that word clearly, or the church about to launch a new ministry, or the church which has little sense of the reality of God in their midst.

The words of Paul to the Romans are likewise clear, "The wages of sin is death, but the gift of God is eternal life through Christ Jesus, our Lord" (Rom. 6:23). The job may take a bit more doing since a figure of speech is involved, but the meaning is clearly to turn around the mistaken idea prevalent in Rome that one can earn eternal life, and that sinning is what is free and easy—a gift of pleasure. The theology is clear, and consistent with the major theme struck in Romans of salvation by grace through faith in Jesus Christ. The figurative language is easy enough to interpret, even with rudimentary verbal skills and a modest acquaintance with Pauline theology.

Seeing the correspondence between the ancient and the contemporary is not always that simple, however. Ernest Best in his book *From Text to Sermon* reminds us of the pitfalls in that journey from then to now. Three important differences separate the worlds: situation, culture and world view.[13]

The *situation* which called forth the writing of Galatians, for example, was the insistence by some of its members that Gentile converts to Christianity had to undergo circumcision. In another epistle, the church at Corinth was troubled by the question of eating meat which had been offered to idols in the heathen temples of that heathen city. Neither of these situations bothers us today. Yet Paul, the writer of both books, is aware that the situation may be the setting for communicating the will of God about wider concerns, of which the particular situation is a specific example. Not only should circumcision not be required for Gentile converts, he wrote, but no other activity, except faith in Jesus Christ. The situation becomes the occasion for God to reveal deeper truth. So also the question of eating meat becomes the occasion for Paul to proclaim the liberty that is God's gift of grace.

The *culture* gap is complicated not only by the distance between centuries but by the two significantly different cultures out of which the Bible rose: the Jewish and the Hellenistic. Perhaps the clearest illustration of both what is meant by culture and the differences between the cultures is in the biblical understanding of personality. Hebraic culture was wholistic in two ways: (1) they thought of personhood in terms of the group, the family, the tribe; (2) they thought of the person as a whole being. The Greek-dominated culture of the New Testament, on the other hand, thought of persons (1) more individualistically, and (2) as separated into body and soul. After Daniel's rescue from the lion's den, for example, those who plotted to kill him were themselves thrown to the lions—*and* their wives and children! The Greek view separating personhood, on the other hand, made possible the antinomian heresy which allowed one's soul to be saved while the body enjoyed whatever pleasures it would. Many cultural postures were common to both the Jews and the Greeks; for example, the belief common to all cultures in the ancient world that God or the gods directly determined the events of nature. There were no secondary causes such as the "laws of nature" or the explanation of weather in terms of cold fronts and sun spots. The crossing of the Red Sea, marvelous as it was, or the healing by Jesus of the blind man, was not nearly so difficult for ancient people to handle as it is for most Americans.

Best distinguishes *world-view*, as a category, as being more personal, more philosophical, more theological than "culture". Judaism spawned several world-views—all within the larger culture of Judaism: the wise man, the apocalypticist, the nationalist. Within Hellenism one could find the Epicurean, the Stoic, the Cynic, the Neo-Platonist, the Gnostic. Standing over against both of these world-views was a third one—that of the Christian community which shared in and stood against the prevailing world-views. Mark's view emphasized Jesus as the Son of God; Matthew, as Messiah. Part of their world-view was determined by their own background; part by the world-view of the people for whom they were writing. Behind each of these phrases about Jesus is a different world view: Jesus "died for our sins," or "in accordance with God's plan," or "for the ungodly," or "to defeat the powers of wickedness." They are not merely random synonyms for the same phenomenon.

How does the preacher help people travel that distance of two or three thousand years when the situations, cultures and world-views are so dissimilar? How and where can we discover the correspondence between the biblical and the contemporary worlds? What factors make it possible?

One is that, to a large extent, we can enter that ancient world vicariously. Studies of ancient languages, of archaeology, of anthropology, all give us insight which enables us to stand, as it were, in the shoes of the ancients. Another factor is that there is a basic continuity of culture rooted in the continuity of the human beings who constitute that culture; made in the image of God, fallen, yearning for a relationship both with the infinite and the finite world. Also, we Christians share with the people of the Bible the experience of a redeeming relationship with the God of Abraham, Isaac, and Jacob, and the Father of our Lord Jesus Christ.

The correspondence between the sacrificial lamb in Israel's ancient sacrifice and the interpretation of it by the writer of Hebrews, may not easily jibe with our own experience of accepting Christ's death on our behalf. Perhaps that correspondence is made with difficulty, but it can be made, the more easily because we sense that our acceptance by God is not our own doing. In some way we may not fully understand, it is made possible on our behalf by Jesus Christ, the Lamb of God who takes away the sins of the world.

We have only hinted at the challenges which face the interpreter who attempts to discover and preach a contemporary Word of God from an ancient book. Correspondence is not an option among interpretative techniques, but a basic principle that will help the one who would preach biblically to overcome those challenges.

4. Polarity

In every biblical passage, opposing forces are moving against each other.

This principle was hinted at in the discussion on intentionality when the advice was given to "postulate the opposite." Material does not appear in Scripture unless there is a purpose which calls it forth: some information missing, some harmful practice going on, some distorted notion of God. The principle of polarity carries that insight further.

The Bible abounds with passages which explicitly set forth poles, opposites, resistances, interfaces, antithemes, dynamic interactions—all synonyms for what we are calling polarity. II Corinthians 5 is a treasure trove of them: earthly tent and a building from God; not unclothed but further clothed; what is mortal swallowed up by life; at home in the body but away from the Lord; walking by faith and not by sight; receiving good or evil. Old Testament narratives set up polarities between Moses and Pharaoh; between Israel and the Babylonian captors; between the vision of Ezra and Nehemiah and the antagonisms of the people in the process of rebuilding the Temple. In Psalm 1 are the blessed man and the wicked. Polarities are not hard to find in most biblical literature, rooted as it is in the story of God and his people, always at odds in one way or another. Indeed, the exegetical task will have turned up a text's polarity simply because the most fundamental literary understanding of the Bible is that it is story—and stories have plots, conflicts, standoffs, tensions, interfaces of people and ideas.

Those forces are easy enough to discover, you say, in some passages but certainly do not appear in *every* biblical passage. What about Psalm 150, which is a straightforward paean of praise to God, with not a hint of any opposite pole? The answer is that polarity in a scripture passage may be either explicit or implicit.

Psalm 150, for example, a psalm of praise, was by its very nature a response to what the worshipers perceived as the goodness of God in their midst, a society permeated by evil, an implicit polarity. Another way of determining the opposite pole is to remember the alienation of Israel from Yahweh in preexilic Israel under the monarchy, the period when most of the psalms were probably written, another implicit polarity.

In the search for polarities, it is helpful to work with a mindset that keeps the interpreter constantly on the lookout for them. The following taxonomy may be suggestive of the kinds of polarities in the Scriptures: (1) *Counterforces*, as in Hebrews 12:1, whose writer urged his readers to "lay aside every weight, and the sin which clings so closely." The polarity here is the energy directing us forward and the energy holding us back. (2) *Ambivalence*, as in II Corinthians 5:5-9: "We know that while we are at home in the body we are away from the Lord," suggesting a desire to be in two situations at the same time. (3) *Logical absurdity,* as in Romans 6:1: ". . . Are we to continue in sin that grace may abound? By no means!" The polarity here is our sin and God's grace cast in a question; if grace is increased to cover greater sinning, shall we sin more to experience increased grace? (4) *Contrast,* as in II Corinthians 5:17: "Therefore, if any one is in Christ, he is a new creation; the old has passed away, behold, the new has come." (5) *Dialogue,* as in the Book of Job in which Job is looking at God's acts with the eyes of faith while his friends are rationalizing God's acts. (6) *Memory,* as in Psalm 137:1: "By the waters of Babylon, there we sat down and wept, when we remembered Zion." The polarity is the memory of Jerusalem in the reality of Babylonian captivity. (7) *Alternatives,* as in I Kings 18:20, 21: "How long will you go limping with two different opinions? If the Lord is God, follow him; but if Baal, then follow him." (8) *Anticipation,* as in I Corinthians 13:12: "For now we see in a mirror dimly, but then face to face." Paul polarizes the partial sight of the present with the eschatological hope in which he will attain wholeness of sight.

These eight are only a few of the many contrasts, comparisons, and parallels that are to be found in Scripture. Perhaps they will suggest a way of reading biblical texts so as to perceive the dynamic elements that wait to be discovered and used in preaching.

A clear notion of the polarity or polarities of the text will both sharpen its meaning and also shape an important step in the preparation of the sermon, as we shall discover in the next chapter.

5. Contextuality

Knowledge of a biblical passage's context or contexts may enhance its meaning significantly.

Every problem-solving activity requires contextual analysis. What else is going on? is the question of the doctor probing the patient's social and occupational context for the causes of an ulcer or hypertension. The parent dealing with a report card detailing a sudden drop in grades for classroom behavior asks about the child's context—in the classroom, on the playground, in sibling relationships, of physical factors like seeing and hearing. The civil engineer designing a bridge needs, among other things, to know the meteorological context of the bridge and commuter traffic patterns.

What is a context? A context consists of all the forces in motion around and upon the text. To put it that way is to eliminate the notion of text as a static entity and to see it as dynamic, moving, pulsating with life.

Visitors to Kodak Park in Rochester, New York, are treated to a telling illustration of contextuality. They stand in a huge rotunda surrounded by photographic displays and artifacts, facing a projection screen probably unmatched in size anywhere. With quadrisonic music as background, the lights dim and on the screen appears a magnificent scene of American western wilderness. In the distance, hundreds of miles beyond the windswept plain in the foreground, stand the Rocky Mountains silhouetted against a brilliant blue sky. The viewer marvels at the expertise of both photographer and film (Kodak, of course) and then discovers that it is only the beginning! Slowly the zoom lens of the projector cuts off a bit of the blue sky, enlarging the mountains ever so slightly. The viewer whose eyes search the giant screen sees a dark spot at the foot of the mountain range. An imperfection in the film? Hardly! As the zoom lens slowly brings the mountain range closer, the dot metamorphoses into a definable shape, a house, a mountain cabin. Now the blue sky is gone, along with most of the mountain range. The cabin's shape is clear—one story, a chimney, a front porch, the figure of a person on the porch. It occupies half the screen, and on either side are trees and bushes which frame it. Now the cabin is big as life, occupying the whole screen, and the figure on the porch, seated on a chair, has given the scene character. He is old, stooped, reading a book. The zoom lens moves in on him more closely. The whole figure dominates the picture, now the head and shoulders only, now only the face, wrinkled and smiling. On his forehead— the size of the speck in that first panoramic shot—another speck. An imperfection in the film? Zoom goes the lens yet farther. It is a fly, an inch wide on the screen, a foot, twenty-feet wide, the tiny striations on the wings now covering the gigantic screen like an abstract painting—a design, wild and wonderful, a piece of God's creation rivaling even the ingenuity of humanity's technological genius.

What the viewer has just seen is text and context. At any given moment, what the viewer sees is "text;" every other scene—before and after—is "context." To view it another way, each item, person, moment, thing, and idea is a text that affects its surrounding context and is affected by it. And note that context is dynamic and not static. The man and the cabin and the mountain (and don't forget the fly!) were technologically limited by a photographic color slide to a moment in time. That does not mean, however, that the context was really static, except for that split second in which the film was exposed. The wind was blowing; the rocks on the other side of the mountain being dislodged by an unseen mountain goat; the man responding viscerally to the story; the fly invisibly exercising wings in preparation for flight. Just so, a biblical text, no matter how ontological or abstract, has a dynamic quality about it. It is as if the biblical writer took a picture in a given instant or even over a period of years, of how it was. The job of the exegete-interpreter is to add to the question what happened and why, the additional questions, what *else* was happening and what effect did that have on the part of the picture now in focus?

The question as to whose context we are dealing with will be covered in greater detail under the principle of identification. The immediate question is the nature of context. What areas does the interpreter search for in investigating the text's context? What else could be going on? The task overlaps somewhat the historical analysis done at the exegetical stage but cannot be overemphasized.

Historical Context. Every biblical text has an historical context; that is, something happened before and after it did. That happening might have been immediately prior, or centuries afterwards. It may have been known to the speaker-writer or not; indeed, it may be known to us and not have been known to him. To Israel, the historical context of Jordan's crossing was the end of the wilderness wandering; it was also the captivity in Egypt, the Garden of Eden, the Exile yet to come. It is all up to the person in the projection booth whose hand is on the historical zoom lens. To take the photographic figure a bit farther, it is even possible to project two images or more onto the same screen and by use of a dissolve unit to see those images as one. Much of the artistic in the work of the interpreter is to choose the limits of the historical context or contexts as they relate to the meaning of the text at hand.

Political Context. Alongside the historical context is the political one. The word political refers, of course, not to any political party or point of view but to the distribution of power in a society. The power of Rome over Palestine was the political reality of the New Testament, from the treachery of Herod to the vindictiveness of Nero. The exile in Babylon was the political context both of the captives who hung their harps upon the willows (Ps. 137:2) and the captors themselves.

What we do not always realize, however, is that "most of the Bible is written from the perspective of the powerless."[14] In *Liberation Preaching,* Justo and Catherine Gonzalez argue that with only rare exceptions Israel found itself under the heel of stronger nations in the great Mesopotamian and Persian area—of Egypt, Macedonia, Syria, and finally Rome. God apparently wanted Israel to be clear that the power is God's power and not Israel's own strength (Deut. 8:1-20). Their point is that oppressed people of our day—women, blacks, citizens of third-world nations—may be able to provide a more accurate interpretation of the biblical word than the white males who operate from places of power in American society.

Whatever the perspective of the interpreter, however, the political realities surrounding the text can bring it alive.

Proximate Context. What is going on in close proximity to the text often provides clues as to the text's meaning. What, in other words, is in the few verses preceding and following the text? In Jesus' conversation with Nicodemus (John 3:1-8), for example, the meaning of "Unless one is born of water and the spirit he cannot enter the Kingdom of God," has long been a subject of debate. Does the passage teach baptismal regeneration, making water baptism a condition for salvation? The principle of proximate context indicates that the conversation had to do with the new birth (spiritual) for which the analogy was the old birth (physical). Nicodemus raised the strange question as to how one could reenter a mother's womb and be born again. Jesus' answer simply referred to water as part of the process of physical birth which he paired with the spirit who makes possible the process of spiritual birth. There is not a hint in the proximate context of the theology of the sacrament of baptism.

Theological Context. How the author or the people around him thought about God affects significantly the interpretation of a text. The theological context of the creation account in Genesis is a world in which monotheism and polytheism were in serious combat. Students of ancient literature are well aware that the biblical account of creation parallels the accounts of creation in other ancient writings, both in general thrust and in many details. It is our knowledge of the theological context that highlights the real importance of the material. What we understand through the theological context is that it was *Yahweh* who created the heavens and the earth, and not the gods of the heathen nations. It is Yahweh who imposed order on the primeval, nonpersonal chaos, signaling the beginning of time. The order of events, the length of days, the location, the relative merits of instantaneous creation versus evolutionary development are questions that have diverted people from the passage's most important meaning. That importance comes to light only when the interpreter understands that the context of the material's writer was theological and not scientific. It is our twentieth-century scientific fascination with the what and the how that may keep us from even asking about the theological context—the Who.

Just so, in the New Testament, one needs to know that the Letter to the Colossians is set in the context of Gnosticism, a kind of syncretistic amalgam of Greek mythologies which set forth a hierarchy of cosmic powers and superior "wisdom". Its influence on the church was subtle but devastating; it apparently was offered as a supplement to Paul's teachings rather than a substitution for it. Paul's countering of it took the form of a brilliant portrait of Jesus Christ as sovereign Lord, God's agent in creation and redemption (Col. 1:15-20). Apart from a knowledge of the theological context, the powerful arguments and scintillating presentation are relatively bland.

Cultural Context. The values of ancient society profoundly affect both the meaning of the text for those who once read it and for us who read it now. In the interface of the biblical world and our own, we need to be keenly aware of the social customs, the family structure, the economic realities, the forms of art and entertainment, and the daily routine of the people who made up the culture. Knowledge of the life of farmers, fishermen, goverment officials, priests and rabbis, women and children, tribal leaders, and all sorts and conditions of people provides the entree to an understanding of the cultural context of a biblical passage. If it was important for understanding the exegetical questions, What happened and why? it is doubly important for the hermeneutical question, What does it mean today? It is precisely the similarities and differences between the two cultures which tend to enable or make difficult the journey between the ancient and contemporary worlds.

To omit or to deal inadequately with any of the above five contexts may keep the preacher from understanding the point of the text at all, or produce an interpretation which bears no resemblance to its probable meaning. Thousands of sermons are preached every week by preachers who develop a clever phrase or use the text as a jumping-off place for an idea they are determined to get across, no matter what. It is through the story of human life touched by God that he reveals himself. The text has meaning only insofar as it is seen as part of that story. James Sanders puts it succinctly: "Biblical preaching in context means re-presenting today the message of a biblical passage for the contemporary context, scoring as closely as possible for the modern hearers the points scored originally by the biblical authors and thinkers in their time."[15]

6. Genre

The literary form of the text profoundly influences its interpretation.

In the last chapter, literary exegesis was prescribed as one of the steps to understanding what the scriptures were saying. In the search for meaning in our world, we are faced with some questions that go beyond literary form itself. Gerhard Lohfink puts it this way: "In the history of the Church infinite confusion and inestimable harm have resulted from the fact that inadequate attention was paid to the basic intent of specific genres and forms. Biblical texts intended as proclamations were thought to be reports. New Testament texts whose purpose was to admonish were thought to be laws. And ecclesiastical texts which had a confessional purpose were regarded as informational data."[16] This concern echoes a theme also voiced recently by Gordon Fee, who notes that this principle is seldom applied in his own evangelical tradition in the interpretation of the New Testament, except for the Apocalypse. "The point is," he writes, concerning the Acts of the Apostles, "that not every biblical statement is the word of God in precisely the same way. The questions must often be: Given that a historical narrative is included in the Acts, *how* is it the word of God for today? Is it merely informative? Does it establish a precedent which is in some way normative? Or are we to elicit a 'principle' from the narrative? Or in the case of the epistles: Is a statement spoken to a given historical context, in response to a specific historical problem, the Word of God for us in precisely the same way it was for them? How, or when, does something that is culturally conditioned become transcultural?"[17] It is to these questions and others like them that the principle of genre addresses itself.

It is easy in dealing with genre to become involved in the debate over how many ways you can slice the Scriptures. Some traditional categories are law, history, poetry, wisdom literature, gospels, epistles, and apocalyptic. Other analyses range all the way from Cline's observation that the Bible is mostly narrative and poetry to Robert Tannehill's minute breakdown of Jesus' stories into pronouncement stories, objection stories, correction stories, commendation stories, and quest stories.[18] Lohfink extends the analytical list with his form-critical categories of prayer, homily, edifying tract, saying, proverb, diatribe, myth, saga, droll tale, legal decision, chronicle, similitude, song, letter, and book of wisdom. Biblical scholars keep turning up new categories and new combinations of categories that enrich our search for the word of God.

Determining the categories, however, is not the end of genre study for the inteperter, but only the beginning. On the assumption that the living God still speaks through the Scriptures, we ask how he speaks to our situation through each of these genres. Take poetry, for example. When the psalmist despairs because God has abandoned him, we conclude that he has accurately and beautifully described how *he* felt at a moment in time. We do not conclude that God has forever abandoned *us* or that abandoning is what he does best. That does not square with either our experience with God or with the witness of the rest of Scripture which tells us that God is always with us, no matter how we feel about him (and sometimes we *do* feel abandoned by God!).

The influence of genre on discovering meaning is further complicated by the facility with which it is possible to shift from one interpretive technique to another *within* a genre. When the apocalypticist writes of a thousand-year period of peace during which Christ will reign upon the earth (Rev. 20:1-6), we know that we are dealing with symbolic language. Some will choose to interpret the material literally, but it is hoped that they will at least acknowledge that they are consciously changing their interpretative technique at that point, since they do not interpret literally the existence, in the same genre, of the "woman clothed with the sun, with the moon under her feet, and on her head a crown of twelve stars [who later] was given the two wings of the great eagle that she might fly from the serpent into the wilderness, to the place where she is to be nourished for a time, and times, and half a time" (Rev. 12:1, 14).

Another example of a more widely accepted shifting of techniques within a genre is I Corinthians 11, part of a Pauline epistle with clear and forthright instructions to the church. The beautiful account of the Lord's supper in verses 17-26 ff is almost universally read aloud and the example followed closely. However, ministers frequently omit verse 30 which attributes some death and illness in the church to participation which does not "discern the body". (Omission is a frequently used and seldom articulated hermeneutical technique.) The church has always been uncomfortable with this verse, and it is seldom mentioned in sermons or Bible lessons. It has been equally uncomfortable with the first 22 verses which prescribe the length of hair for men and women with Paul's observation that "nature teaches" that long hair is degrading to a man. What does he mean by "nature?" In what way is it degrading? And how long is "long"?

One further example: the account of the descent of the Holy Spirit at Pentecost (Acts 2:1-21), which is a strange narrative indeed. Is it literal history, an origin story, or theological drama? There is a sense in which it is a kind of reversal of the Genesis story of the confusion of languages at Babel; now, by the power of God, the languages are suddenly intelligible! It is also a "feast story" with a reverse twist; a celebration of the law vs. the celebration of the coming of the Spirit. It could be any one of these options—or a combination of some sort. The fundamental issue for the biblical preacher, however, goes beyond choosing among those options or the questions which they raise: the issue is the normativeness of the account. How is this the word of God for us? Is this the normal way the Holy Spirit comes upon believers, as a large and growing segment of the church believes? Does the preacher move automatically from what *was* to what *ought to be?* Is the *descriptive* automatically *prescriptive?*

You may answer yes or no in this case. Your answer may depend largely on the ecclesiastical tradition in which you were nourished —upon your presuppositions. Perhaps your interpretation need not be justified beyond that. But suppose you are a person who has become a Christian in your mature years and come at the question more or less freshly. You have no experience with ecstatic language in the church, but neither do you discount the possibility of it as an authentic gift of God. From other New Testament books we gather that undisciplined, uninterpreted speaking in tongues became a divisive force—indeed a scandal—in many places, as it has among Christians in our day. You know something about it but are still not sure that it is God's will. Suppose we go around the issue and not face the question as to whether the event happened exactly as described, or even whether it is normative. Suppose we look for the "deeper meaning." In that case the meaning might revolve around the significance of the Holy Spirit who restores communication in the church and who gives us the strength to carry his word to a needy world, as did those on whom the Spirit fell. Or, if it is a reverse twist on the Old Testament celebration of Pentecost, the sermon might lift up the freedom of the Spirit as over against the strictures of the law. And surely there are other possible meanings.

The point of the illustration is that while the determination of the text's genre profoundly influences its interpretation, it certainly does not happen in any automatic way. One cannot say that even if it can be established that an event happened as described, that event or something like it ought to keep happening. To put the question another way: are we to find *truth* only in accounts which communicate *fact?* Turn it around: because a genre, say historical narrative, establishes the factualness of an event, does it carry with it the expectancy that it is a true pattern for us? In a well-authenticated historical event, Samuel quoted God ("Thus saith the Lord!") as commanding Saul to destroy the Amalekites—"both man and woman, infant and suckling, ox and sheep, camel and ass" (I Sam. 15:3). Did God really say that? If he did, was it God's will only at that time because the Amalekites were so terrible and deserved to be wiped out? Or was that action justifiable only in a theocracy but not justifiable in a modern democracy? Is genocide a pattern which God would approve for today, under certain circumstances? What would those circumstances be? Does this passage justify the slaughter at Mai Lai toward the close of the Viet Nam war? Or shall we skirt the issue of factualness and normativeness, and deal with the passage as a case study in obedience, which it certainly *is!*

What may be more helpful is to link the principle of genre with the expectations that were set out for the whole enterprise in the first place. What we can expect of the Bible is that it will (1) reveal the human situation apart from God, (2) record the gracious nature and activity of God, and (3) evoke a response from its readers. The question is, which *theological* function does this genre of literature perform at this particular place? Samuel may have "heard" the Lord telling him to pass on an order for the merciless extinction of an entire nation. We who read that account evaluate it, however, as a distinctly ungodly commandment sandwiched between the clear law of Moses, "Thou shalt not kill," (Exod. 20:13) and the tender picture of Jesus who gathered children around him—in all three Synoptic Gospels, by the way (e.g. Matt. 19:13-15). The necessity of placing a particular text in one of these theological functions is a weighty one, but it is at the heart of the whole interpretative enterprise, as we shall see even more vividly in the next chapter when we begin to put the sermon itself together.

7. Language

Knowledge of the role and use of language facilitates the discernment of meaning.

One of the most valuable insights of the "new hermeneutic" is its emphasis on the text as "language-event." The juxtaposition of these two words suggests the power that is in language. It is not anything new, of course, to say that language has power: that is known to every human being in relationship with another. The concerns of both Gerhard Ebeling and Ernst Fuchs, seminal thinkers in the "new hermeneutics" school of thought, lift the principle of language to that of prime importance in understanding the Scriptures. To Ebeling, a language-event is not "mere speech" but "an event in which God himself is communicated."[19] He is concerned that we not use language to speak *about* reconciliation, but to *reconcile*. He rightly calls us not to "understanding *of* language, but understanding *through* language.[20]

Both the presuppositions and elaboration of the new hermeneutic's view of language raise serious questions about its conclusions, but it has provoked biblical interpreters into a useful study of the role of language. Their starting place is the Bible itself, which is permeated with accounts of the power of language and, more importantly, is itself in its own powerful language-format the embodiment of language-power. "And God said . . ." is both the literary thread of the creation account and the power of creation itself. The Epistle of James records the power of the tongue, "a restless evil, full of deadly poison. With it we bless the Lord and Father, and with it we curse men, who are made in the likeness of God" (James 3:8, 9). It is language, says Paul in Romans 10:17, that enables Christian faith: "So faith comes from what is heard, and what is heard comes by the preaching of Christ."

What constitutes language? How can the interpreter move toward meaning through discerning its role and use? Four elements inform that search: the meaning of words, grammar and syntax, abstraction, and figures of speech.

The meaning of words is extremely important information for the interpreter. Discovering those meanings has a high priority in the

exegetical process. Like the principle of contextuality, it overlaps the
hermeneutical process. A central figure in the Old Testament, for
example, is the judge. An understanding of his role in the
community of Israel becomes far clearer with the knowledge of the
word's meaning. A judge functioned, not as a black-robed official on
an elevated courtroom bench but as a leader of his people. His work
combined the decision-making power of a Supreme Court justice
with the work of a police officer—constantly moving among the
citizenry—and a social worker who helps people to adjust their lives
to their situations.

Another element of using language to find meaning is grammar
and syntax, already defined in the last chapter. The richness of these
disciplines may be seen in the oft-used biblical phrase, "the word of
God." It is clearly a genitive construction, but is it subjective genitive
or objective genitive? If it is subjective, it lifts up the God who is
doing the speaking; that is, God is the subject of the action—he it is
who speaks the word. If it is objective, God is the object of the word.
The word has the action, to point to God. The word is not so much
from God as it is *about* God. In the grammatical distinction lies the
richness of the preacher's work. He or she speaks the word that is
about God; but, more profoundly, speaks the word that is *from* God,
enabling God to speak his own word.

The third factor in dealing with language as an interpretive tool is
the abstract-concrete scale, or ladder. Sermonic language is
frequently and justly criticized for being too abstract, for failing to
touch down at the realities of life. It is full of words like love,
compassion, justice, right and wrong, happiness, evil, etc. General
semanticists illumine the relationship between abstract and concrete
words by placing them along a vertical continuum with abstract at
the top and concrete at the bottom.

Place the word "compassion," for example, at the top of the scale. As
a mid-level abstraction, place "helping neighbors in need." As a
low-level abstraction, write "emptying your grocery shelves for the
stranger across the street whose house was fire-bombed by bigots." That
is compassion in the concrete. The importance of knowing how to deal
with the abstractional ladder becomes obvious as we move through the
rest of the principles and techniques of interpretation.

Abstract

High-level abstractions

Mid-level abstractions

Low-level abstractions

Concrete

Figures of speech constitute the fourth dimension of language concerns for the biblical interpreter. There are those who argue that all language is figurative, that language by its very nature is symbolic. That is certainly true, but there is equal agreement among most students of language that figures of speech can be readily distinguished from literal language. We know, for example, that when Jesus refers to himself as the bread of life (John 6:35) that he is speaking figuratively. Figurative language represents one concept in terms of another, building on a mutually understood analogy. Interpretive problems arise when (a) the mutuality of understanding does not exist, and (b) when it is not even agreed that the phrase is a figure of speech in the first place. Jesus' words, "This is my body" (I Cor. 11:24) precipitated one of the greatest debates in church history, a debate fundamentally about whether he was using figurative or literal language.

The scriptures abound with figures of speech. Some of the more common ones are figures of:

Comparison. A *simile* expresses resemblance with the use of "like" or "as". "Like the glaze covering an earthen vessel are smooth lips with an evil heart" (Prov. 26:23). A *metaphor* is an implied comparison, the suggestion of a resemblance. "I know that you are obstinate, and your neck is an iron sinew and your forehead brass" (Isa. 48:4).

Association. Metonymy involves one word in place of another because one suggests the other. In the story of Lazarus and Dives, Abraham says of the rich man's brothers that "they have Moses and the prophets" (Luke 16:29), meaning that they have the writings of these men. A contemporary example is the newscaster's "The White House said . . ." *Synecdoche* involves the use of a part for the whole or a whole for a part. Joel warns his listeners to prepare for the final battle in the day of the Lord—to "beat your plowshares into swords, and your pruning hooks into spears" (Joel 3:10). The parts are the instruments of battle; they stand for the whole.

Intensification. One method of achieving the intensification of an idea is *irony*. An excellent example is the admonition of Joel just referred to. He reverses the figure used by the earlier prophet, Micah, (Mic. 4:3) who saw God's people going to Jerusalem on a mission of peace. Having fallen yet again from God's favor, he gives Micah's words an ironic twist, saying that they must now go to battle and to death. Figures of speech may therefore be used in more than one way. *Hyperbole* is another kind of intensification; it is conscious exaggeration. Spies brought back to Joshua the word that Canaan could be conquered: "The people are greater and taller than we; the cities are great and fortified up to heaven" (Deut. 1:28).

Personalization. Some writers and speakers use *apostrophe;* they address persons or forces who are not present as if they were. "O my son Absalom," David cried, "my son, my son Absalom! Would I had died instead of you" (II Sam. 19:4). In *personification,* a thing, idea, or quality is represented as a person. "The sea looked and fled, Jordan turned back. The mountains skipped like rams, the hills like lambs." (Ps. 114:3, 4).

Understatement. When an idea is too direct or powerful for a given situation, a less powerful word is sometimes used, a *euphemism.* As in our own language, euphemisms are generally used in the Bible for sexual or excretory functions. To "come near" or "to know" another usually means, in context, to have sexual relationships with that person. Judas was referred to in the discussion of his successor as one who had "turned aside, to go to his own place," (Acts 1:25) certainly a euphemism for the torments of hell!

These figures are simply a few of the more frequently used language devices in the Scriptures with which the interpreter needs to become acquainted. Among less frequently used figures are ellipsis, zeugma, aposiopesis, meiosis, pleonasm, and epanadiplosis. [21] While a knowledge of these figures is no guarantee of instant meaning, the skillful interpreter cannot function without it.

8. Identification

Meaning is shaped by the placement of one's self and one's hearers in the dynamics of the text.

To work with this principle, one has first to perceive the dynamic quality of the biblical story. It is probably best seen in the principle of polarity, in which forces are seen to be moving against each other; two persons in conflict, two cosmic forces in battle for a person, one person attempting to reconcile two others, God and a man in dialogue, etc. Sometimes it will be remembered, those forces are explicit in the text; at other times they are implicit.

The interpreter's question is, where do I see myself in that plot and how does my congregation fit into the encounter? Is it the church that is being addressed? The world-systems of our day? Believers? Unbelievers? Unbelievers who think that they are believers? To the extent it can be discovered and articulated for a given situation, the word of God is the constant; the recipient is the variable. But who is the recipient?

The easiest mistake to make in identifying one's self with the text is to see it as a model for morality rather than a mirror for identity. This distinction is made clearly and provocatively by James Sanders in his *God Has a Story Too*. With rare exceptions, there are no moral models in the Bible. Joseph in Egypt comes close, viewed as he is through ancient wisdom literature. But the Sunday School heroes were full of moral holes: Abraham with his lies about Sarah; Jacob, the deceiver; adulterous King David; every one of Jesus' disciples. Indeed, one way of viewing Jesus himself is not so much a model to be followed but as one against the measure of whose life our lives look sick. We are not called primarily to be imitators of Christ but recipients of his forgiving grace.

The hermeneutic technique which leads people to seek heroes is that of static analogy, "a box of jewels of wisdom forever of static value;"[22] in Sanders' language. It tends to be used by people who are comfortable with understanding the Bible as a set of propositions. To them, the interpreter's job is to discover, classify, and apply those propositions to life. The homiletics books written in that tradition usually have sections on "application," as if the congregation were passive students, come to learn lessons about God and then to put them into practice in their daily lives.

"Dynamic analogy," on the other hand, calls our attention to the ongoingness of the biblical story. God is still alive in his world, in his church, re-presenting the biblical drama through preaching. The congregation is not listening for "lessons," but identifying with the characters—their situations and their destinies. Listeners are being pulled into the action—coaxed onto the stage, as it were—to participate themselves in the drama of redemption.[23]

Another easy mistake is always to make our identification with "the good guys." We hear the ancient prophets railing against the wickedness and vice of the big cities, and we nod our heads in agreement at what everybody already knows, that there is evil in the big cities in abundance. What we miss is God's word to us that there may be evidence of illicit kissing right under our own noses and of thievery in our income tax file folder.

Sanders says, "Dynamic analogy means we can read a text in different ways by identifying with different people in it. For example, if we always identify with Jesus in the passage in Luke 4, his sermon at Nazareth, then we will read the last verse of the pericope (Luke 4:30) wondering how Jesus managed to escape that awful crowd. How marvelous! But if we read the passage again, identifying with the good folk in the synagogue, Jesus' relatives and friends of his hometown, and see how he so sorely offended them that they tried to lynch him, then by the time we get to verse 30 we ask an entirely different question: How did the scoundrel get away?"[24] They did not want to hear that when Elijah, the great herald, comes he would bestow his blessings not on the hometown folks but on strangers, even on enemies. Another group became angry at Jesus' story about the apparent injustice of paying the same wages to those who worked one hour as to those who worked all day. Yet is this not the essence, the scandal of the gospel, that God gives freely, lavishly to those who do not deserve his love—to people like us?

Catherine and Justo Gonzalez help us to look at the identification process in still a different way, using this same parable to illustrate: "When we imagine a group of Chicano migrant workers, waiting at the appointed place to be hired, perhaps, for the day, the parable begins to look quite different. For those who frequently find no work, for those who never know in the morning if there will be any wages at the end of the day, the parable would communicate the great justice, not the unfairness of God. The congregation needs to see this, and by so doing, the absent powerless will be brought into their midst."[25]

A more traditional way of working with identification is to choose one person in a narrative with whom to ask the congregation to identify, like the younger brother in the parable of the prodigal son (Luke 15:11-32). One might even identify with each of the three characters in a series of sermons, or even within one sermon. The possibilities are endless. What is important is that, even if no particular identification is worked out in advance, the story be told so compellingly that each listener will become involved in the action—as a recipient of God's favor.

Sanders offers a simple guideline for working with the principle of identification: "Whenever our reading of a biblical passage makes us feel self-righteous, we can be confident we have misread it."[26]

9. Multiplicity

A text may yield a variety of meanings.
The illustrations given through the discussion so far embody this principle quite vividly. The story of Pentecost, examined in the section on genre, suggests how the determination of the form of the material offers several possibilities as to the text's meaning. The nuances of word meanings, grammar, and syntax also extend the variety of meaning possible in a text. In many texts, there are two or more polarities from which to choose; the meaning of the text may well depend on the choice made. With which character or idea in the biblical material shall the interpreter identify? How wide is the context within which the text will be viewed? Which of the several contexts is chosen?

Perceptual differences related to differing cultures also support and illustrate this principle. Charles Kraft relates the story of "a group made up of Africans and missionaries (who searched for) the main point of the story of Joseph in the Old Testament. The European missionaries all pointed to Joseph as a man who *remained faithful* to God no matter what happened to him. The Africans, on the other hand, pointed to Joseph as a man who, no matter how far he traveled, *never forgot his family*. Both of these meanings are legitimate understandings of the passage," Dr. Kraft concluded, "But differing cultural backgrounds led one group to one interpretation and the other group to the other interpretation."[27]

Interpretive technique is another factor that may produce a variety of meanings. Take, for example, the bronze serpent episode in Numbers 21:9. "So Moses made a bronze serpent and set it on a pole; and if a serpent bit any man, he would look at the bronze serpent and live." In Jesus' conversation with Nicodemus (John 3:14, 15), he used the interpretive device of *typology*, making himself the antitype of the serpent in the Old Testament: "And as Moses lifted up the serpent in the wilderness, so must the Son of man be lifted up, that whoever believes in him may have eternal life." If one views the episode through the technique of *heilsgeschichte*, or salvation-history, it may be seen more broadly as one episode in a continuing story of God's salvific works, from the beginning to the end of the Scriptures.

Isaiah preached, "The wolf shall dwell with the lamb, and the leopard shall lie down with the kid, and the calf and the lion and fatling together, and a little child shall lead them" (Isa. 11:6). The interpreter may view the passage using the interpretive principle of *prophecy-fulfillment* and conclude that it is essentially eschatalogical; the prophet sees God's shalom at the end of the age when the violence of nature's enemies will be no more, and even a child can cope with life's most severe testings. Others will choose to interpret the text *messianically* and see that little child as Jesus of Nazareth, the Child himself, whose leadership alone will bring ultimate peace to the world.

To list these interpretive techniques is not to advocate or to defend their use in any given case—nor is it to eschew their usefulness. Detailed guidelines and warnings are available in material which goes beyond the scope of this primer. It is to say that in the incredibly complex task of biblical hermeneutics, the interpreter ought to be relieved from the anxiety that each text has only one correct meaning and that either woe or heresy is the consequence of missing that meaning. In the possibility of multiple meanings, actually, lies much of the richness and the challenge of engaging in biblical interpretation.

10. Perspective

The Bible is a witness to the saving activity of God in Jesus Christ, the meaning of whose life, death, and resurrection controls the meaning of every passage.

How many messages can be preached from the Bible? What a silly question! On the surface of it, the answer is clear and obvious—hundreds, thousands, lifetimes. Perhaps. To look at the question another way, the answer is one—only one. In one form or another, every authentic Christian sermon proclaims that Jesus Christ rose from the dead to offer eternal life and to establish justice in the world. Karl Barth is supposed to have responded to an American reporter's question as to how he might summarize his theology, "Jesus loves me, this I know; for the Bible tells me so." Paul wrote to the Corinthians: "God was in Christ reconciling the world to himself " (II Cor. 5:19). The Gospel of John puts it in a few words: "For God so loved the world that he gave his only Son, that whoever believes in him should not perish but have eternal life" (John 3:16).

Preachers are tempted to offer lessons in Christian living instead of helping people admit that such lessons as they have learned have been useless to them apart from the transforming power of the gospel. Having exegeted a difficult text, they are tempted to guide people to meaning which may or may not point them to the risen Christ and the power of the Holy Spirit in God's world. They may offer three reasons for giving generously to missions; four aspects of prayer; two ways the church can change the power structures of society. They may offer a rationale for the defection of Jesus' disciples and warn listeners not to forsake him; explain the meaning of the angel with the key to the bottomless pit; lift up as our example

King Josiah who did what was right in the eyes of the Lord. None of this is preaching biblically in its fullest sense.

To preach biblically is to announce the recovery of our identity as sons and daughters of God, created out of nothingness by the gracious act of God, rescued from Egypt, astonished and energized by the inexplicable power of the risen Christ at our table. It is to declare firmly that Jesus Christ attends our future—in the family rooms and board rooms and locker rooms of the week to come, and in the locked rooms that we open to him with such great reluctance. Biblical preaching does not academically set forth four aspects of prayer—or three or five-and-a-half—but points to the Christ who sits at the right hand of God making intercession for us. Biblical preaching does not highlight the sterling character of King Josiah, but exalts the God who gave him wisdom and energy to do what was right in the eyes of the Lord.

Is there no room in biblical preaching then for "the dark side of God?" Are preachers not false to their own prophetic tradition if they omit God's warning of judgment? Are there not times when biblical preaching scolds? Let James Sanders put this question into perspective.[28] There are two basic kinds of hermeneutic, Sanders says, constitutive hermeneutic and prophetic hermeneutic. Constitutive hermeneutic is supportive; with the prophet Nahum it says, "The Lord is good, a stronghold in the day of trouble; he knows those who take refuge in him" (1:7). Prophetic hermeneutic thunders out of the next verse, "But with an overflowing flood he will make a full end of his adversaries, and will pursue his enemies into darkness" (vs. 8).

Just as these two kinds of hermeneutic appear side by side in Nahum, so also do they coexist in the entire Bible. But they do not point to two sides of God, as if God were a two-headed theological monster, sometimes loving and sometimes hating. The constitutive word is for listeners who need to hear about the God who cares for, loves, undergirds, supports, and acts in mercy toward his people. The prophetic word is for those who have heard that message and rejected it. It is the word of wrath and judgment by the God who has been scorned—whose power to guide his people through the wilderness is matched by his power to send them back into exile. The distinction is clear in our own idiom when we speak of the preacher's task to comfort the afflicted and afflict the comfortable.

The preacher of our own day works in that same tension, always attempting to be sensitive to the listener's needs. At *all* times, at the core of the preaching, is the good news of God's gracious offer in Jesus Christ. At *some* times, the preacher lays out the consequences of rejecting that offer—of judgment, or what Luther called "God's strange work."

To call for perspective is not to excuse anyone from the tough, puzzling, demanding, and sometimes frustrating, work of biblical interpretation. It is not to paste a Jesus label on every sermon manuscript page, sometimes to woo people and sometimes to scold them; it is not quite that simple. Preaching Jesus Christ from an Old Testament text, for example, demands most careful handling. Converting legal material and moralistic texts into occasions for preaching grace is a sensitive and difficult task. Dealing with paradoxes and outright contradictions takes deep study and sanctified common sense; it also requires the principle of perspective.

One of the oldest axioms in biblical interpretation is that we interpret the parts by the whole and the whole by the parts. To say that is to articulate in another way the principle of perspective. The whole of the Bible witnesses to the promise and fulfillment of redemption; the parts of the Bible hold meaning insofar as they witness to that wholeness in God's plan.

The principle of perspective also allows us to say about some biblical material, "You can't get there from here." At some point in time, every interpreter comes to a text that defies interpretation and has apparently defied generations of commentators, if success is judged by agreement among their interpretations (try Exod. 4:24-26, for example). If, after prodigious and prayerful labor, you and every scholar you read simply cannot discover how this passage witnesses to God's creative and redemptive work in his world, remember that the Bible is full of texts that witness magnificently to the God who makes transparently clear to us more of his will than we are ready to do.

These ten principles constitute both a hermeneutical system—a theoretical rationale— and a series of practical questions that can be put to a passage of Scripture. Their ultimate purpose is not to understand a book, but to understand the human situation our listeners bring to the hearing of the Word and to enable them to respond to the gospel—the gracious, saving Word that is at the center of the Scriptures.

IV. A METHODOLOGY
FOR BIBLICAL PREACHING

The intention of the last chapter was to set forth some principles for moving from what the Bible *said* to what the Bible *says*. To that end a set of principles was offered for the interpretation of Scripture. With that set of principles, it may become possible to arrive at an intelligent conclusion about a text's meaning for today.

Another way of working with a biblical text to arrive at meaning for today—a way that brings us more directly to the actual preparation of a sermon—is to utilize a conceptual framework, a construct, a model. To do this is not by any means to eschew principles of interpretation—the ones in the preceding chapter or any other set of principles; it is to utilize those principles in a focused way—to seek out the building blocks of thought with which to shape the emerging sermon. Is there a single model which would pull together *all* the necessary elements for bringing a text from the "then" to the "now" in such a way as to facilitate preaching of the gospel? and, if so, what would it look like?

Any model we might produce would certainly have to utilize the techniques of exegesis and the principles of interpretation. It would have to provide for an honest engagement with the biblical text and an equally honest facing of life as the listeners are living it out. A model would have to take seriously the theological dimensions of the material at hand, placing the gospel—the work of God—at its center, but taking into account the doctrine of sin and also the ethical consequences of the gospel. The model ought also to recognize and utilize the dynamic of the biblical story, the encounters of people and ideas. It ought to facilitate the formulation of a central idea that will control the selection and arrangement of the sermonic material, but it should not, however, be primarily a homiletical model that might make all the sermons it produces sound alike; it should engender variety rather than uniformity. Such a model would also be integrative, i.e., it would enable the preacher to incorporate into the sermonic material to be used the wide variety of data and insight in the theological spectrum—Christian ethics, mission, evangelism, sociology, communications, and other disciplines along with the classic disiplines of biblical studies, theology, and church history. It ought, finally, to be time-effective; to be a lifting of the demanding burden of sermon preparation rather than one more item on an already long agenda.

Does such a model exist? One is reminded of the little boy in the back row of the classroom drawing a picture with such diligence that the teacher inquired what he was portraying. "I'm drawing a picture of God," was his answer. "But no one knows what God looks like!" the teacher replied. "They will when I'm finished!" he retorted. One must not carry the analogy too far, but this chapter does make the attempt to build just such a model, one that fulfills all those expectations.

It is in a set of expectations with which we have to begin, the very set of expectations set up in chapter 2. We expected from the Bible that it would (1) reveal the human situation apart from God, (2) communicate the gracious nature and activity of God, and (3) evoke response to God's word about himself and his world. On this three-fold structure the dyadic model unfolds. It is "dyadic" in that it is composed of six dyads, or interfaces each one of which makes its unique contribution to the model.

As it unfolds, two of the ten principles of interpretation emerge immediately to help shape what we shall do; the principles of polarity and of correspondence. The principle of polarity says that within each text—or in the text as perceived in the context—is an encounter between the text's dynamic forces. On the one hand is the human situation apart from God, human need; and on the other, the action of God to meet that need by his participation in human affairs. That encounter is graphically portrayed in Dyad 1. The other basic polarity in Scripture is the response of humankind to God's gracious action in his world; that is Dyad 2. The principle of correspondence posits a relationship between that ancient world and our own; that relationship is communicated in Dyad 3.

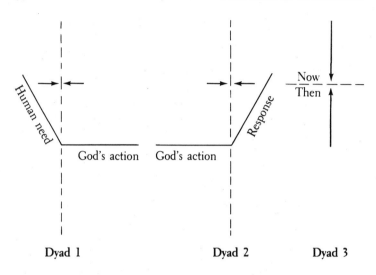

Dyad 1   Dyad 2   Dyad 3

HUMAN NEED

We begin with humankind as the first step in our analytical task because this is the area in which we have the most data to work with; because it is the closest at hand; and because it is what brings us to the task in the first place. We live inside our own skins and relate daily to other human beings. When we read the Bible, using the principle of identification, we relate to other human beings who, like us, have loved and fought and celebrated and cried and grown tired and achieved—in short, have participated with us in our humanness.

What is the human need that forms the first element of the model we are constructing? In the Scripture, it is portrayed in a staggering variety of ways: as sin, as transgression of the law, as conscious choice to defy the living God; as being under the judgment of God because of the alienation our ancestors chose and we continue; as question, revealing our lack of information about the will and purposes of God; as ambivalence in moral dilemmas; as sickness of the soul; as participation in tragedy; as fallen from grace. Theological literature is not lacking in synonyms for the need of humanity apart from God.

The starting place, then, for developing a hermeneutical model for preaching is to investigate the text for whatever expression of human need may be found there. Behind that search is the whole body of what is called biblical anthropology, the study of humankind. Two basic affirmations constitute that branch of theology: one is that people are created in the image of God (Gen. 1:26) and are therefore good; second is that people's lives are characterized by sin (Rom. 3:23) and are therefore in need of salvation.

The prophets in the Old Testament excel in their statement of human need. Page after page details the woes of the human race, the unfaithfulness of the people toward Yahweh, the dire consequences of their rebellion. In the New Testament, Jesus was brought to tears over Jerusalem, and again at the death of his friend, Lazarus. Paul chastized each church to which he wrote for a different combination of failings. At the time of the book of the Revelation, the human need was the response of God's people to persecution by the emperor. At all times, people have acted with imperfect knowledge of God's will and purpose.

One important exegetical consideration at this first step is locating the human situation properly within the "history of religion"; both with the event itself, and with the event as it was transmitted and recorded for a later generation. One of Jesus' sayings, for example, may have addressed the anger of the Pharisees on the day following the Sabbath, but the account of that conversation may have been useful to an ancient Gentile church gathered for worship in a quite different (though not opposing) way. To achieve maximum power in preaching, the preacher—for good and sufficient pastoral reasons—will probably select one of those standpoints upon which to build the sermon.

In investigating human need, we utilize yet another principle, intentionality, the area of human need that God's spirit intended to address in the writing and the canonization of the Scripture text at hand. Paul Tillich's theological method of correlation begins by asking questions of ultimate concern.[1] Harry Emerson Fosdick puts it this way: "Every sermon should have for its main business the head-on constructive meeting of some problem which [is] puzzling minds, burdening consciences, distracting lives."[2] In his famous essay, "How We Think," John Dewey says that reflective thinking begins with the definition of the problem.[3] Every physician learns that treatment cannot proceed without both diagnosis of the ailment and its etiology—the cause or causes that produced it.

The preacher looks diligently, then, for the *why* of the text's existence. It may be explicitly stated in the pericope; it may be implicit, needing to be dug out by addressing appropriate questions of the text; it may be found in one of the text's many contexts. If the text is worth preaching on, the human need is there awaiting discovery and articulation.

The principle of correspondence now comes into play from another perspective. It says that there is a basic continuity in the human experience. What this means is that the preacher is dealing with two sets of people who have in common an alienation from God and from each other: the people whose lives are chronicled in the Bible and the people who are sitting in pews on a Sunday morning. What makes it possible to preach to them from the Bible is that they share a common humanity. The task now becomes to find the corresponding areas of their lives that await the gracious entrance of the redemptive power of God. That relationship constitutes a fourth dyad.

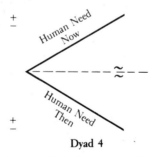

Dyad 4

The plus and minus symbols, both in the then and the now, stand for the wholeness for which God intended us at creation and for our chronic failure to embody it. We are at all times a mixture of those positive and negative forces.

The mathematical symbol of similarity separating the then of the Bible from the now is an important one in understanding the dyadic model. Its viability with regard to any text ranges from clear and obvious to highly debatable. It is at this point that the matter of probability comes into play. Take, for example, "For all have sinned and come short of the glory of God," (Rom. 3:23). One can conclude with a high degree of probability that our congregation, and we ourselves as preachers, share with the Romans and every person who has ever lived the qualities of sinfulness. But when we read: "Behold, I was brought forth in iniquity, and in sin did my mother conceive me" (Ps. 51:5), we are faced with a number of interpretive problems, several points down the probability scale. Facing and dealing with those problems necessitates a serious wrestling with the challenging problems of correspondence.

In the actual use of the model, to be exemplified in the next chapter, the preacher will write out a clear statement of just what the then and now problem areas are. In his *Manual on Preaching* Milton Crum sets forth a most helpful method for arriving at this statement. In either text or congregation, or both, find the "*symptomatic behavior* which needs to be changed by the gospel . . . a concrete example of our fallen, sinful behavior . . . on the feeling and/or actional level (so that) a listener can say, 'That's me; I behave that way,' without fear of condemnation." Secondly, "get at the *root* of the symptomatic behavior under focus . . . the beliefs and perceptions which underlie the behavior (so that) the listener can respond, 'That's me; that's what happens when I behave that way.' "[4] While the examples are in first person singular, the procedure certainly applies to the handling of problem areas in the church as a community or in the world.

A series of corollary questions may also be useful in investigating the human pathology indicated by the text and its correspondence in the contemporary world. How does the need look, feel, smell, sound, taste? Where, how, when does it occur in human life? Where are its parallels in Scripture, in contemporary literature, in sermon literature, in the personal experience of myself or of others? Who most dramatically embodies it? How do I or we participate in it? Where do people observe it in today's newspapers, magazines, on radio and television, in novels, in movies?

What should be obvious by now is that the very process of defining the human need merges into the process of fleshing out, of surfacing illustrative material for the sermon. That is as it should be; no search for illustrations is worthwhile if they are to be tacked on to a disembodied homiletical proposition. Worked at this way, the materials of the sermon should provide an embarrassment of illustrative riches at the very earliest stages of conceptualization.

What may be less obvious is that the procedure being described is not so much homiletical as hermeneutical; that is, it is not being advocated that treatment of the human situation should occupy the early moments of the sermon itself. For Fosdick, that *is* the expectation. He is supported in studies on the order of presentation in public speaking which suggest that it is better to present the problem before offering the solution.[5] Nevertheless many sermons, both biblical and creative, come at the task quite differently and quite effectively. The task is also hermeneutical, in that the search for understanding depends on the authentic identification of the interpreter and of the intended audience with the concern being addressed.

Two questions now present themselves: (1) with which do we begin, the now or the then? and (2) what if no correlation can be found?

It does not matter in which world the preacher begins the task. The text of the lectionary, ecclesiastically prescribed or one's own, provokes the biblical preacher to thought and prayer about the now-world. Also, the questions and failures of our congregants and ourselves remind us of the ancient peoples and the word from God they alternately accepted and rejected.

Inhibiting our discovery of a correlation between then and now may be the low-probability relationship occasioned by the nineteen centuries that span the two worlds. The biblical situation may speak to our culture only at a somewhat higher level of abstraction, a distancing that generally weakens the message. In addition, many ethical dilemmas and ambivalences have arisen in our complex and technological culture that defy analogy with the culture of the biblical world. What story, injunction, command, or principle informs a decision whether to begin a baby's life in a petri dish?

In those cases, we go to the Christian social ethicists for such guidance as they may be prepared to offer, or we deal with the questions at high, and somewhat questionable, levels of abstraction.

THE NATURE AND ACTIVITY OF GOD

The second expectation we have of the Scriptures is that they will reveal to us the gracious nature and activity of God. The adjective "gracious" is an important one, because of the breadth and focus of its root, grace (*charis*). Its very common use in the New Testament covers a wide variety of meanings but comes to focus in Pauline theology where the entire human experience of God in Christ is expressed in terms of grace. "For by grace you have been saved through faith; and this is not your own doing, it is the gift of God—not because of works, lest any man should boast." (Eph. 2:8, 9). The first section of the dyadic model prepares for this second one, God's gift of himself, his favor, his eager love. We shall also call this step the *good news* and the *gospel*.

This step in sermon preparation lifts up both the nature and the activity of God, neither of which would, alone, provide the theological completeness needed to undergird every preaching event. Statements about the nature of God tend to be abstract, removed from listeners' families, work, and relationships; statements about the activity of God may easily get disconnected from the ontological.

It is obvious that not every text will provide, in itself, an explicit theological statement of this sort. In most cases, the preacher will use the principle of contextuality to discover the theological stance of the writer, and to go beyond that immediate theological context to see how the passage at hand relates to the whole counsel of God.

To avoid the sermon's becoming a mere scolding for the congregation's sins of commission or omisson, perhaps coupled with some good advice on Christian living, the second, and central step must become the fulcrum on which the whole enterprise turns. Indeed, it is precisely the omission of this step in sermon preparation that is at the root of the theological malaise in most congregations.

To omit a statement of who God is and what he is doing is to miss the point of the story, to leave out the power by which people can deal with their need. Inattention to the text's theological base almost inevitably leads to moralistic preaching.

Pursuing the principle of correspondence, we divide this theological quest into the two worlds to which God reveals himself: the world of the Bible and the world of our times, the fifth dyad. While it is the same God who reveals himself to essentially the same kind of people, we do well to articulate that revelation at two points in the model, the then and the now. The words may be identical, or they may embody the truth of God in then language and now language. The important thing is that the good news for this sermon, based on this text, be written in and not left to the chance hope that it will somehow come out in the preaching.

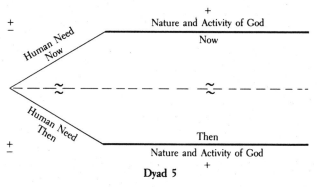

Dyad 5

Note that the symbol for similarity persists into the second stage; it represents the interpretive principle of correspondence, based on the theological assumption of the continuity, the eternality of God. Note also that the central section of the model is characterized by a plus sign denoting the positive input of God's being and work in the arena of human need. God's revelation of himself, to put it another way, is always consistent with his perfect nature.

Two caveats are important at this point. First, this theological statement should embody God's word of grace as primary, with any word of judgment or chastisement as secondary. There is no doubt that God's nature involves his justice and that he is frequently seen to act in judgment; both Old and New Testaments are permeated with the theme of God's judgment. What is important to remember is that judgment is always secondary and derivative, a consequence of the human rejection of God's grace; and that it is motivated by God's love. The word offered in Christian preaching, therefore, is always the word of grace, tempered by warning in those instances that are called for by the text or the context.

Second, the author's perception of God may be severely limited. Every Old Testament text is, by its nature, incomplete—from our specifically Christian perspective. That is not to say that the Old Testament is any less the Word of God than the New Testament; indeed, the insights of many Old Testament texts are richer than those of many New Testament texts. It is to say that the preacher may wish to employ more than one text to round out the theological base for the sermon. The very existence of multiple texts in the lectionary for each Sunday provides a precedent for so doing.

Could we call this second step the gospel? Yes and no. If the gospel is defined purely as *kerygma*, the recalling of God's messianic promise, the proclamation of the death, resurrection, and exaltation of Jesus with the summons to repent and receive forgiveness of sins (Acts 2:14-38), then the answer is no. In how magnificent a *variety* of ways God revealed himself throughout the thousand years between the opening and closing of the canonical Scriptures! If, on the other hand, the kerygmatic proclamation is both the theological under-girding of the entire biblical account and its grand culmination, then the answer is yes. Whatever God reveals of himself is good—not always comfortable or pain-free—but good news and, in that sense, the gospel.

A final word, perhaps unnecessary, is that the form of the theological statement must match the form of the human need statement. If the sermon is to have coherence—not to mention theological integrity—salvation must be matched with sin; reconcili-ation with alienation; gospel with law; the water of life with the thirst of the soul; hope with persecution; life with death; justice with oppression; light with darkness; release with guilt; and so on. Preachers will find a good dictionary of antonyms to be an indispensable homiletical tool.

THE HUMAN RESPONSE

One cannot hear the word of God without responding to it. In one way, the Bible may be understood as a record of the human response to God's word. For the children of Israel, the word came in the command of Pharaoh to Moses: "Rise up, go forth from among my people, both you and the people of Israel; and go, serve the Lord, as you have said" (Ex. 12:31). From that point on, the history of Israel was a history of their response to the deliverance by Yahweh through his servant Moses. Jesus began his ministry with his intention to proclaim liberty to the captives (Luke 4:18, 19); the Gospels describe the response of both his followers and the rest of the people to this word. At Pentecost the Holy Spirit made his power available (Acts 2:4); the book of Acts and the Epistles chronicle the church's response to that event.

Just so, each text calls forth response. In some cases, it is possible to articulate that response historically; in most, we can only guess, or we can move to the context to indicate how that word was received. In most instances, however, we know what the *intended* response was—our study of the text's intentionality tells us that. We also know, by now, how we want our hearers to respond to the word for today we have articulated in our model. We want people to utter a responsible yes to the God who has given us his message; to begin to live in God's light, to repent of their sin, to take hope in the darkness of economic dislocation, to fight for justice in society, to pray with a deep sense of God's presence. The articulation of the response completes the dyadic model.

As with the first two sections of the model, there is a similarity between the two worlds—a sixth dyad. How could it be otherwise? God's word was that he would provide for his children in the desert journey to the promised land: they followed, but with what a mixed response! Jesus' audiences heard and understood; some followed while others plotted to kill. The Holy Spirit came with extraordinary power; and some "kept my word and have not denied my name" (Rev. 3:8) while others wound up "wretched, pitiable, poor, blind, and naked" (vs. 17). A safe prediction is that persons who hear us preach will constitute an equally mixed bag of response.

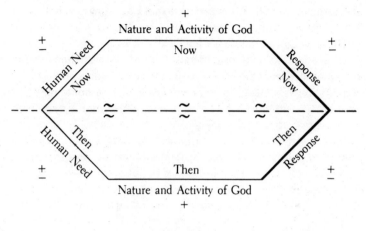

+
Nature and Activity of God
Now

+
–
Human Need
Now

+
–
Response
Now

≈ ≈ ≈

Human Need
Then

+
–

Response
Then

+
–

Then
Nature and Activity of God
+

Dyad 6

In the chapter on exegesis, our approach to the exegetical task was to search the Scriptures with a common interest in our future. This task, the task of laying out the intended response to the good news, brings us full circle. When the last word of the sermon has been uttered, the last hymn sung, the final prayer offered, the people who have heard the word are saying as they did following Peter's sermon at Pentecost, "What shall we do?" (Acts 2:37).

The desire to *do*, laudable as it is, needs to be balanced with the desire to *be*, to become "a new creation in Christ" (I Cor. 5:17). That distinction helps us to handle the response section of the model. Just as our initial concern for human need made us look at both the symptoms and the root of our alienation; and our search for God's word to us focused on both his nature and activity; just so, we preach to effect a response in both the activities of being Christian and the inner changes wrought by the Spirit through the word.

What if the text gives no hint about the actual or the desired response? The broadest, most highly abstract response one can call for is the understanding and doing of God's will; that is the response, in general, for every sermon. Historical narrative does not call for any specific response at all—nor does a psalm, a genealogy, a parable, an apocalyptic passage. And, sometimes, a direct command is so removed from tradition that we do not know how to handle it: "If I, then, your Lord and Teacher, have washed your feet, you also ought to wash one another's feet" (John 13:15).

Unless one wishes to deal literally with Jesus' injunction to wash one another's feet and have a basin and towel handy, the call for response must be made at a different level. That response may be a relationship with the One whose life exemplified humility, perhaps in a particular act of stooping love. Fundamentally, the very statement of the gospel will determine its own response, whatever the genre. To put it another way, the God who reveals himself through his word also works through his Spirit to put that word into action. What *could* happen, the preacher asks at this point, as a result of an honest encounter with the God who is revealing himself through this text?

The preacher needs to be most careful that the question does not lead to moralizing, even to giving the impression that one's own being or doing can lead to acceptance by God or the achievement of his redemptive purposes. To that end, it is best to avoid moralistic words in the statement of the response; words like "should," "must," and "ought."

Another concern is honestly to match the response with the need. The injunction of I Thessalonians 5:18, 19 is to pray constantly and to give thanks in all circumstances. On the ladder of abstraction, "all circumstances" takes in a lot of territory. One might make a clear, accurate theological statement about the risen Christ who connects us with the Father in prayer. Stating the human need, however, is tricky. One could put in all sorts of human need about which we could pray. Faithfulness to the text, however, makes us identify the need as the Thessalonians' deep concern for "the times and the seasons" of Jesus' second coming. (I Thess. 5:1). If there is no liberty to move up the abstractional ladder to address to a variety of human needs the injunction to pray constantly, then we could use this particular text only when our congregation is in a state of confusion about Jesus' second coming. That would severely restrict its use—perhaps eliminate it entirely—for most congregations. To match the need and response, the preacher needs to generalize the uncertainty, perhaps to our presumed and idolatrous "need" to know in advance what God is going to do. That concern fits nicely into the "all circumstances" in which we are enjoined to pray, but it is neither so specific that it does not fit our situation nor so general that it has no focus.

Both the theological and homiletical integrity of the preaching event call for checking the relationship of response to need: a positive response should, in some way, cooperate with God's action to relieve the need.

CENTRAL, CONTROLLING IDEA

One of the most hallowed homiletical axioms is that the preacher should be able to put into one sentence the essence of the sermon. That sentence is called the sermon's thesis, proposition, generative idea, big truth, subject sentence, sermon-in-a-nutshell, or main point. Here it is called the central, controlling idea to indicate that it is not only to be heard as the most important idea in the preaching event, but that it controls all the other ideas.

Composition of this idea is extremely important to the sermon's integrity; that is, the unity that pulls together the diverse elements that impact the hearers—main points, rhetorical questions, stories, theological arguments, newspaper quotations, and the like. The central, controlling idea is not an option but an urgent necessity.

To say this is not to insist that the central, controlling idea be heard early in the sermon as a kind of syllogistic premise that will be proven by arguments and evidence. Especially if the sermon development is narrative, it may not be heard in so many words at all. Like every other part of the dyadic model, this element is to be used primarily for clarifying the theology and thought structure that undergird the actual sermon composition. At the same time, the composition of a central, controlling idea may be extremely useful homiletically if one chooses to build the sermon outline on it.

How does one determine the sermon's central idea? It will certainly arise from the theological section (the nature and activity of God) or the response section or both. It may even include a word or a phrase from the human need section, to set the gospel or the response in perspective.

How does one know if the statement of the idea will really do its integrating work? Make it (1) accurate, authentically reflecting the true intentionality of the passage; (2) dynamic, containing truth in compressed form which is awaiting release; (3) relevant, clearly tied to the concern that motivated the sermon in the first place.

THE DYADIC MODEL: A PERSPECTIVE

The task proposed at the beginning of this chapter was an ambitious one. We set out to put the principles of interpretation and the techniques of exegesis into a graphic form that would move us close to the actual process of sermon composition. We set up a number of conditions to be met if the model were to work. It is now time to look at that ideal and at the reality.

The task of exegesis is represented in the lower half of the dyadic model; it reconstructs, as much as possible, what happened and why. To that task are addressed the various analytical skills of the exegete: historical, literary, and theological. The dotted line which separates the then from the now is the hermeneutical bridge. Along its length are three signs of similarity representing the journey between Jordan and Peoria; a journey fraught with exciting and sometimes frustrating problems. Along the top are the evangelical, pastoral concerns that connect the family of God in churchly pews with our spiritual ancestors out of whose life came the record of need, revelation, and response.

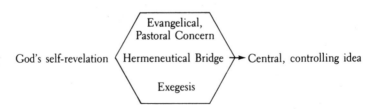

Some of the principles of interpretation permeate the whole model-building process: the principles of *simplicity, genre, language* and *multiplicity,* none of which matches the dyadic model step-for-step, but all of which impact it. The principle of *intentionality,*

however, directly informs the area of response. The principle of *correspondence* is what links the two worlds separated by time. *Polarity* becomes obvious with each move from one step to another: the need and its resolution; the offer of God's grace and the human response to it. The preacher is constantly exploring the text's *contextuality* after having determined where its materials fit the model. Dealing with the *identification* among self, audience, and the original hearers makes preaching possible. And it is the principle of *perspective* that places the statement of the gospel at the center of the model.

The formation of the dyadic model should by now have demonstrated that it does provide for an honest engagement with the biblical text and an equally honest facing of life as the listeners are living it out. In the statement of human need, the doctrine of sin is laid out; in the statement of a desired response, the ethical expression of the gospel. The model helps to formulate a central idea by requiring the articulation of each fundamental element in the sermon's underlying thought structure, but it does not force that idea—or any other element—into a homiletical structure.

The model serves an integrative function in that each theological discipline can inform one or more of its elements. Christian ethics, for example, is best represented by the response-now phase of the model; it investigates how people respond to the claims of the gospel. Missions and evangelism specialists perceive their mandate in the needs of the world, derive their message from the gospel, and do much of their research in the area of response through studies of society and world culture. It is the study of sociology of religion which gives us significant insight into the human need now, as well as to the various ways people respond to their understanding of God at work in this world. Communications students identify with the dyadic model as a communications model that takes seriously the source of communication (God's self-revelation), the analysis of the audience (human need), and the phenomenon of feedback (response). The classical theological disciplines feed into the content of the model the insights of biblical history and language, the process and categories of theology, and the sense of perspective that church history brings to any religious enterprise.

Is working with this model time-effective? Each preacher will have to decide that personally. Students who have worked with the dyadic model, both seminarians and continuing education participants, have found it so since it provides pegs on which to hang virtually all biblical literature and to see it in viable relationship. Arranging the playing cards by numbers and suits does not guarantee victory in gin rummy, but it significantly enhances the possibilities of winning, and it does speed up the game!

The dyadic model is, in some ways, unique. Actually, it is just another way of stating what effective biblical preachers have always done: they have spoken to people's need; they have announced the good news of Jesus Christ; and they have called for decision.

The dyadic model is also rooted in classic Christian theology, most pointedly in the Heidelberg Catechism, Question 2: "What points of doctrine must you know in order to live and die happily in this faith? Firstly, how great is my sin and misery; secondly, how I am saved from all my sins and misery; and thirdly, how thankful I must be to God for such salvation."

Recent writers on preaching have put the same basic ideas into their constructs. In *Preaching Law and Gospel*, Herman Stuempfle builds his entire theology of preaching around the concepts of law, gospel, and obedience: the transgression of the *law* which constitutes human need, the *gospel* which stands at the center of our model also, and *obedience* which we have named response.[6] Heinrich Ott, successor to Karl Barth at Basel, said it this way in *Theology and Preaching*: "In principle the sermon as a whole has just these three things to say. Its centre lies in the middle point, in the proclamation of God's action. But in order to be intelligible and effective, this proclamation needs the other two parts, the disclosure of the true situation and the emphasis on the resulting obligation."[7] Milton Crum's "Dynamic Factors" are five, but they encompass the dyadic model perfectly: symptomatic behavior, the root of that behavior, the unhappy resulting consequences, the gospel content as an alternative to the old way, and "the new results which follow the new way of believing and perceiving which the gospel provides."[8]

Perhaps the most important contribution of this book is to redirect the preacher's attention to the nuts and bolts of the task: the fundamental, stripped-down list of exegetical hard work to be done; interpretive principles to be wrestled with; sentences of the dyadic model to be written out, and all of it checked for completeness, coherence, and accuracy.

THE HOMILETICAL TASK

The craftsmanship of the sermon has not been the task of this book; that work is amply discussed in the other books of the Abingdon Preacher's Library, as well as in a myriad of books on preaching in and out of print. The question is certainly being asked, however, how do you use the material discovered in the dyadic model for preaching?

The answer is to use it intelligently, sensitively, and especially pastorally. The prime determinant, in fact, of what material to use and how to use it is pastoral. If, for example, a congregation has a long tradition of scriptural disuse, years of Sundays given over to preaching on popular topics of the day with scant reference to the riches of Scripture, the preacher will want to introduce healthy amounts of material from the biblical side of the model. Or, if one's own preaching tradition, or that of the parish, is so heavily weighted with the life of Jesus and Paul's missionary journeys that the worshipers have rarely been asked to think about social injustice as perceived by Jeremiah and minority Christian leaders of our day, then one will preach accordingly.

The preacher may elect to place heavy emphasis on scriptural material in a given sermon, feeling that it has the power to carry the message to a contemporary audience with little or no conscious bridging effort. Another reason to do this might be that the particular human need being addressed is so sensitive, it is better to come at it obliquely. On the other hand, one may wish to touch only lightly on the scriptural material, especially if the authority of the biblical revelation may be taken for granted, or the biblical material is very well known. The point is that it is not the *quantity* of time given to the exposition of the Bible that determines whether the sermon is biblical, but the *quality* of its faithfulness to the biblical message and its evocation of the biblical memory.

That pastoral sensitivity should also lead the preaching pastor to examine with the congregation just what needs they perceive in their individual and communal life and what life-style they would like to achieve as a result of hearing the gospel week after week.

How does the dyadic model determine the sermon outline? The answer is that it is not intended to, but that it may. The model is not—to repeat—homiletical; it is hermeneutical. But it does suggest at least one popular mode of organization, the problem-solution sequence. After an introduction, the preacher could simply transfer the need and gospel steps to the two main points of the sermon, and handle the response in the conclusion. A bit more complicated is a six-point sermon which might organize the six sections of the dyadic model in any one of hundreds of mathematical combinations. Another way of working would be to begin with the central, controlling idea and support it with illustrative material from the biblical text and from the life of the community, creatively interspersed. The preacher might adapt the material to a first-person format to tell the story based on a plot explicit in the story or even on one's own plot. If one works hard enough at it, one might even find three points in alliteration!

The abundant recent writing on both theology and sermon as story raises the question as to whether we really can separate so neatly the then and the now of biblical preaching. It is an important question, particularly if one wishes to avoid the kind of pedanticism to which such a model as the one we have been discussing could easily lead. One way to come at this question is to visualize the model as being set up on a horizontal, cork bulletin board, the shape of it determined by a rubber band set in place with an immovable bolt at the far left point, four thumb tacks helping to form the hexagon and the central, controlling idea pulling at the right side. If the central idea is dynamic enough, it will pull the entire enterprise with force enough to pop loose those four thumbtacks, and the rubber band will vibrate down the middle with the then and now elements resonating as one. That accomplished, the two worlds will function together as God intended them, the ancient word speaking to the modern world, and the modern world listening to the ancient but living Word.

V. A CASE STUDY

Three tasks remain: (1) to develop an instrument by which the preacher can apply the insights developed in the chapters on exegesis and interpretation; (2) to demonstrate how the dyadic model works, using a single text; and (3) to offer some guidelines for sermon development on texts of various literary genres. We shall combine the first two tasks by showing one way to approach a text for preaching. In chapter 6, we shall offer some suggestions for interpreting other kinds of texts.

To offer a complete exegetical study of a biblical text would go beyond the scope of this brief volume. What is presented is a sample worksheet providing the categories in which the preacher may do anything from making simple notes on the passage to doing the kind of extensive study required for a pastors' study group or for a seminary course on biblical preaching. The comments offered in this worksheet are on the simple end of that continuum, using Joshua 1:1-9 as a sample text. The comments offered are just enough to define the category by example and to suggest the direction to be taken in a more detailed study.

I EXEGESIS

Selection

Church Tradition: Message for New Year's Eve Family Night Service not provided in lectionary (day on liturgical calendar may be indicated here).

Need of Congregation: Transition from one year to another evokes some anxiety every year; looks like especially difficult year ahead, especially controversies about selective service and threat of World War III.

Literary Integrity: A cohesive paragraph; clear carryover from

Deuteronomy 34; single encounter of Yahweh and Joshua; final verse summarizes and focuses paragraph.

Text and Translation

Textual Analysis: No significant problems.

Translation: (Here the exegete will indicate choice of translation and/or make own translation from original). The Revised Standard Version seems an adequate translation.

Literary Exegesis

Genre of Book and Text: Historical narrative with a strongly theological thread. This text is direct discourse, one-way from Yahweh to Joshua.

> *Form-Critical Insights:* Material probably originated in victory songs that were modified into prose.

> *Source-Critical Insights:* Songs probably came out of cultic worship rather than the campfire.

Structure of Literary Unit:

1. Historical setting (1, 2a)
2. Command to conquer Canaan (2b)
   a. Description of territory (3, 4)
   b. Assurance of success (5)
   c. Exhortation to strength and courage (6, 7a)
   d. Exhortation to obedience of the law (7b, 8)
3. Closing affirmation
   a. Exhortation to fearlessness (9a)
   b. Promise of Yahweh's presence (9b)

> *Redaction-Critical Insights:* Material edited into book form around late seventh or early sixth century, B.C. Unifying theme is that God has always carried out his promises and expects people to respond in obedience.

Language of the Text: Style suggests use in covenanting or coronation ceremony (note similarity to Joshua's commissioning in Deut. 31:23).

Historical Exegesis

Authorship: Edited by theologically sophisticated person with strong concern for obedience.

Audience: Immediate audience for God's words was Joshua; presumably also for refugees from Egypt at Jordan's edge; and succeeding generations.

Location: East bank of Jordan—precise location unknown.

Date: Probably 1250–1200 B.C.—possibly 1450–1400 B.C.

Setting:

Political Setting: Canaanite cities dominated lives of all. Hebrews from Egypt were joined by others who had fled oppression for a rural life. Object was to take each city, since Canaan had no central government.

Cultural Setting: Canaan had been technologically and artistically advanced, but now in decline. Hebrews never allowed to forget they were lower class outsiders in a feudal culture. Being prepared for war was a constant in that society.

Religious Setting: Shrines at Gilgal and elsewhere important in this period. Faith in Yahweh strong. Early Yahwism was inclusivistic, believing in worth of all people; antedated later cultic, exclusivistic religion.

Theological Exegesis

Systematic: Strong element of *covenant*, the promise of God conditioned by the obedience of Israel.

Situational: God perceived as creator/sustainer of all peoples throughout earth, preceding later, narrower view of God, and foreshadowing New Testament God of Gentile world.

Historical: Succeeding generations saw conquest variously as 1) vindication of their warlikeness and 2) reinforcement of their experience of God in their midst. In today's heightened sensitivity to oppressive structures, we view Israel as an oppressed people who are freed but who then become oppressors themselves, a not uncommon phenomenon in world history.

II. INTERPRETATION

Presuppositions

About God: God is essentially loving, caring, always at hand in best and worst of life. His expressed love for Israel (and us Christians) may tend to blind us to his unexpressed love for the Canaanites (and persons of non-Christian faiths).

About Human Nature: People tend to stumble and blunder into new circumstances; they cope poorly apart from connections with the divine. deepest human anxiety is the absence of God.

About the Bible: Biblical story is paradigmatic of human life, revealing God authentically when sensitively understood.

From Christian Experience: Many personal tragedies lived through have strengthened my relationship to God, heightening my awareness of his presence at all times.

Principles

1. *Simplicity*

    Obvious meaning is God's presence and power in times of transition and especially at threat of war. The oppressed-turned-oppressor motif must be faced—within this sermon, or at a later time.

2. *Intentionality*

    Text communicates reality, faithfulness, and activity of Yahweh: (1) at time of conquest, (2) to sixth, seventh century B.C. readers, (3) to us today.

3. *Correspondence* (situation, culture, world-view)

    Our precise situation is gathering to look toward the unknown of the new year, remembering God's care in the old year; mixed feelings of gratitude and anxiety much the same, especially about possibility of international conflict. Cultures vary widely, but differences compensated for by situational similarity. Hebrew-Christian world-view sees divine purpose in events, life-stages, rites of passage—not celebration of New Year for emotional release.

4. *Polarity* (interpreter makes a "grocery list" from which one

or more polarities will eventually be chosen to shape the dyadic model)

Divine *and* human dimensions

Memory of Moses *and* promise to Joshua

Egypt *and* Canaan

I was with Moses *and* I will be with you

No man (antagonist) *and* God (protagonist)

Obedience to the law *and* turning to right or left

Meditation on law *and* having it depart out of your mouth

Being frightened *and* being strong/courageous

5. *Contextuality* (historical, political, proximate, theological, cultural)

(Here the interpreter checks against exegetical findings the meaning for today that is emerging and begins to choose that context which has the most promise.) Especially striking is the insight from *cultural* exegesis that oppression and militarism pervaded life. The context of the family facing the threat of war and loss of life emerges out of reflection on that situation.

6. *Genre*

(Literary form has already been established by exegesis. At this point, interpreter determines how that form helps to determine the meaning). Direct, divine discourse, in context of historical narration, is revelation at its most powerful. Form does not call into question the theological affirmation of God's faithfulness.

7. *Language*

Word Meanings: God *will not fail* (1:5), lit., "let drop" or "abandon." *Be strong and very courageous* (1:6, 7, 9), lit., "make every exertion." *Have good success* and *prosperous*, (1:8), lit., "do wisely, behave with forethought."

Grammar and Syntax: Nothing remarkable.

Abstract—Concrete Language: Highly abstract language, will have to work at concretizing.

Figures of Speech: Synechdoche in 1:3, "sole of your foot" and 1:8 "book of the law shall not depart out of your mouth." Hyperbole in 1:5, "No man shall be able to stand before you;" 1:7, "to do according to all the law;" and 1:8 "meditate on it day and night."

8. *Identification*

As the father of a draft-age son, I scare easily at the current war talk. I identify with the apprehension of my peers in the church and of the youth who wonder what the coming year will bring. I also remember World War II, Korea, and Viet Nam, and the strength provided by God through separation, death, and disaster.

9. *Multiplicity*

A wide variety of sermons could come from this text, depending on polarity and the context chosen. Any of nine polarities could produce a distinctive sermon.

10. *Perspective*

Interpretation will be "constitutive hermeneutics," offering support in time of need. The early Yahwist theology fits neatly with the inclusivistic Christian view of God's all-pervading presence (cf. Matt. 18:20). One parallel is Christ's commission in Matt. 28:16-20; another is the resurrection appearances in John 20 and 21.

III. FROM TEXT TO SERMON

Dyadic Model

The initial stage of the dyadic model may include a large number of ideas that emerge from reflecting on the processes of exegesis and interpretation. Some preachers title seven blank pages, one each for the six steps in the dyadic model and the seventh for the central, controlling idea, for recording all the ideas that come to mind. Much of the sermon's power lies in compaction of the ideas into sentences that are lean, spare, and pointed. The process of sharpening is perhaps the most challenging phase of sermon preparation. On the facing page is the result of distilling into one model the vast number of ideas that came out of the exegetical and interpretative process followed in working through the Joshua text.

The Dyadic Model

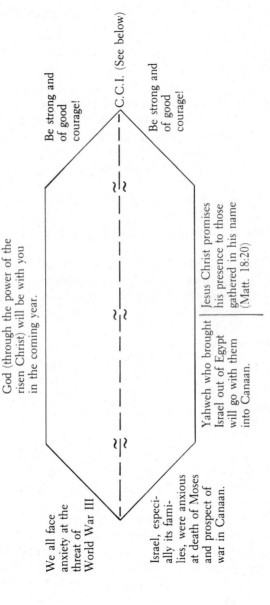

We all face anxiety at the threat of World War III

God (through the power of the risen Christ) will be with you in the coming year.

Be strong and of good courage!

C.C.I. (See below)

Be strong and of good courage!

Israel, especially its families, were anxious at death of Moses and prospect of war in Canaan.

Yahweh who brought Israel out of Egypt will go with them into Canaan.

Jesus Christ promises his presence to those gathered in his name (Matt. 18:20)

C.C.I. However uncertain—even threatening—the new year may look on this New Year's Eve, we enter it courageously and in the strength of the God of Joshua—and of Jesus Christ—who goes with us.

Sermon Design

Introduction: Several thousand eighteen-year-olds registered
with Selective Service this year. You may not have noticed
unless you are one, or have one in your family. The prospect
of going to war is the context for tonight's text.

I Will the new year plunge our country into war?

    A. Israel at Jordan knew that they faced war (re-create the
situation).

    B. We have only the apprehension, the anxiety about it.

    C. But a deeper anxiety is that God will forsake us.

II Whatever the year holds, God promises his presence.

    A. God never forsook his people (examples).

    B. He gives evidence of his care and strength among us today
(examples)

Conclusion: God's word to us is so clear and so powerful that it
is said three times in the text, "Be strong and of good
courage." God give us ears to hear it every day of the year to
come, and the will to live by it. Amen.

OBSERVATIONS:

The above case study is, in the briefest possible compass, an
example of how one might go about the preparation of a biblical
sermon on an Old Testament text. The process differs from working
with a New Testament text basically only in the two-step articulation
of the central, theological section. At that point, it will be noted that
the "nature and activity of God" line in the dyadic model was
bifurcated to show a corollary New Testament text or concept in
order to insure that the sermon is rooted in Christology. As the
sermon design developed to the point recorded here, the
christological element was not strong, but it could easily become an
important part of the sermon's development.

Note also that in this text the three basic elements of the dyadic
model were clear and obvious. A text will not always articulate all
three steps. In that case, one must go to the context to find the
missing elements or discover them by implication.

It may also be noticed that much of the material turned up in the exegetical study and the application of the principles of interpretation did not find its way into the sermon design. The completed sermon might incorporate some of the insights from the study, but the value of the research lies in the abundance of material form which to choose sermonic material, the confidence level with which one preaches, and the storehouse of data for another sermon to be preached later on that same book of the Bible, subject matter, or era in biblical history. For this reason, the preacher ought to file not only the sermon outline or manuscript but the worksheet as well.

The articulation of the central, controlling idea is indispensable for insuring the integrity of the sermon. Many times the very statement may be used as the conclusion of the sermon. In this case, it is restated, although it could easily be used as is for the sermon's conclusion.

The choice of the "impending war" theme was somewhat arbitrary for this case study, but it grew out of the preacher's personal involvement in the issue and his pastoral perception.

This sermon design is a simple one, attempting to deal more or less evenly with the biblical and contemporary worlds. Pastoral considerations may, however, influence the preacher to dwell more on one world than another. The preacher might choose to deal with the text as story, using a narrative approach. Perhaps one could begin with the response to which God calls us, "Be strong and of good courage," and proceed inductively to the situations in which we need to hear that word and then back to the biblical account. Alternatively, the preacher could begin with the provocative statement that our deepest anxiety is the absence of God and then go any one of four or five ways. Sermon design is a matter of the preacher's creativity, but exegesis and the principles of interpretation provide the data with which it is possible for him or her to *be* sensitive and creative!

VI. GUIDELINES FOR
PREACHING BIBLICAL GENRES

Historical narrative, the literary genre from which the case study of chapter 5 was drawn, comprises the most extensive collection of material in the Scriptures. Several other literary categories, however, appear in the Bible's pages, each one of which requires a somewhat different approach to the exegetical, interpretive, and preaching tasks. This chapter suggests ways of approaching some of the more familiar biblical genres.

NARRATIVE

Narrative material is not only the most extensive but the best known of biblical material; it is also probably the easiest to preach. The reason is that stories have identifiable characters who are like us; we can readily become involved in the dynamics of the event. To preach narrative material well requires especially keen insight with regard to identification. Using the identification principle developed in chapter 3, the preacher must make sure that listeners see themselves as persons of need who are encountered by the living God.

Epic narratives comprise one main type of narrative. These stories cover the broad sweep of history like the exodus of the children of Israel from Egypt, the whole of David's reign, Nehemiah's memoirs, the life of Jesus, and the early years of the church. All too seldom does a preacher attempt a sermon on an epic narrative: and all too poor is the congregation that has never glimpsed the larger picture within which many of the encounter stories take place.

Encounters similarly enable listeners to identify themselves with persons needing and receiving the gifts of God's grace. The encounter of Elijah and the priests of Baal took a short time, but it was a pivotal event in God's revelation of himself. So also were the encounters between Jesus and the Pharisees, between Philip and the Ethiopian eunuch. *Short stories* are limited in time span but are stimulating vehicles for the larger story of the movement of God into the human story. Ruth, Jonah, and Esther are all short stories whose characters can come alive through imaginative preaching. *Parables* are commonly attributed solely to Jesus, but they were widely used methods of communication in the Semitic world and can be found in such Old Testament books as Ezekiel, Jonah, Hosea, and Isaiah. They may either have a single point, provoke thought, evoke an array of feelings, or simply make the listener squirm. *Origin stories*, like the Garden of Eden, Babel, and Moses at Sinai, are narrative explanations of how things began—the world itself, languages, and the Law. *Signs and wonders*, sometimes called miracles (but never in the Bible), constitute unusual acts of God in his world: the healing of Naaman in the Jordan, the restoration of sight to Bartimaeus, and supremely, the empty tomb. *Theological narratives* also make marvellous preaching material. The books of Samuel and Chronicles join the Acts of the Apostles in this category. *Sagas* are short units of Scripture, dealing with a single episode in a family's life affirming for readers the value of membership in God's family.

The most important guideline in dealing with narrative material is to keep the human participants in the stories in the human-need category of the dyadic model and not to let them slip into a hero role. As fine a woman as Ruth was, her story was recorded and preserved in canon, not as an example of filial piety, but as a refutation of the excessive zeal of Ezra and Nehemiah that would exclude Ruth and all foreigners from God's favor. Who belongs to God? is the question the book raises. The answer is that God chose a foreigner, Ruth the Moabitess, to be shown the favor of a prominent Jew of Bethlehem, to be the means of continuing the family line that would produce King David and Joseph, the carpenter, and Jesus of Nazareth. The good news is that God's idea of who is in his family is much bigger than ours, and that he is still inviting us "foreigners" to his love, to become resident in Christ's kingdom.

POETRY

Poetry comprises the second largest category of biblical literature. Readers of the Bible usually identify poetry exclusively with the

Psalms, but it actually pervades the Bible. Nearly one-third of the Old Testament is in poetic form. Unlike Western poetry, which is characterized by balance of sounds and phonetic rhythm, biblical poetry involves a balance of thought, a rhythm of ideas. It is written out of a deep urge to share, and expresses itself in a highly condensed form in which the choice and order of words convey its power. The interpreter is primarily concerned with conveying emotion rather than historical data or theological nuances. Identification with a character is important only occasionally; identification with a feeling is central.

The Psalms is one of the Bible's longer books and is exclusively poetic. Old Testament scholars differ in the number of categories, but some of the most commonly agreed upon categories are hymns, enthronement psalms, psalms of lament (both individual and community), songs of confidence, thanksgiving psalms, royal psalms, imprecatory psalms, wisdom psalms, pilgrim songs, and liturgies. *Poetry of the prophets* comprises the whole of Obadiah, Micah, Nahum, Habakkuk, and Zephaniah, as well as large sections of Isaiah, Jeremiah, and several other prophets. Song of Songs is a *love poem*, and the entire book of *Proverbs* is in poetic form.

Poetry is more widespread in the New Testament than is generally realized, with many hymn fragments finding their way into the epistles. The book of Revelation contains the largest proportion of poetry in the books of the New Testament, and even the Gospels contain poetry, mostly quotations—echoes of the Old Testament poets.

Preaching from poetry involves primarily the conveying of feeling. It is not to say that the sermon on a poetic text does not require exegetical and hermeneutical study; it is to say that the wide range of feeling expressed in biblical poetry needs to be handled and categorized with unusual sensitivity. Take the imprecatory psalms, for example, like Psalm 137, that ascribes happiness to those who kill the babies of the Edomites. It is important to understand the terrible anger and desire for revenge of the psalmist whose agony in captivity must have rivaled the painful torture of modern political prisoners. Certainly God's word through the psalm, however, is not identical with the curse of the psalmist. Rather, the preacher dealing with this text tries to capture the desolation of those who are separated from their homeland and from the Temple that is no more. What is true and good is that Yahweh was there to hear them raise their community lament and their hope, however dim, that in his own way and time he would restore the Temple to its rightful place in the community of Israel. The principle of correspondence makes it possible for us to identify the psalmist's deepest woe with our sense of distance from God, and to understand ourselves as we pronounce our own brand of curses on those we blame for that separation. But the very fact that the words are formed, that we remember with joy the Lord's song, is the hope that is our message to preach.

The interpretive question in dealing with poetry is whether this poem, or the part with which we are dealing, helps to illumine the human situation, to communicate the good news, or to define and evoke response. The theological function of Psalm 137 is to help us understand and articulate our situation—our grief and anger at that which separates us from God. The poetry of Isaiah 61:8 has a different function; to tell us who God is and what he is doing.

> For I the Lord love justice,
>   I hate robbery and wrong;
> I will faithfully give them their recompense,
>   And I will make an everlasting covenant with them.

Jesus' poetry, familiarly called the Beatitudes, fulfills our third expectation—the response section of the dyadic model—by poetically describing what it is like to have discerned the will and purpose of God:

> Blessed are you poor, for yours is the kingdom of God.
> Blessed are you that hunger now, for you shall be satisfied.
> Blessed are you that weep now, for you shall laugh.
>   Luke 6:20-21

In preparing a sermon on poetry in the good news or response mode, the preacher completes the element or elements of the dyadic model from the context, especially the theological context, to keep the text in perspective.

LAW

Law is the third traditional category of biblical literature. There are single laws which are either conditional or categorical; they have to do with terms under which slaves may be bought and released (Exod. 21:2-6) or with causing injury or death (Exod. 21:12-14). There are also *smaller collections* of laws such as the Ten Commandments (Exod. 20:1-17), sometimes called the Decalogue. The *larger collections* of laws are generally called *codes:* the Covenant Code (Exod. 20:22–23:33), the Deuteronomic Code (Deut. 12–26), and the Holiness Code (Lev. 17–26). Some Old Testament scholars also refer to the Priestly Code as a fourth type, but material ascribed to this category is scattered throughout the Pentateuch and does not have as strong an integrity. The Covenant Code contains forty-one laws, about half of which deal with crimes against persons and property, with the others legislating on cultic practices, slavery, judicial proceedings, resident aliens, usury, and aid to an enemy. The Deuteronomic Code sets standards for the centralization of worship, slaughter, kingship, cities of refuge, and a variety of other matters. The Holiness Code majors on sex crimes, priestly regulations, seasonal feasts, and other cultic concerns.

Very little of this Old Testament material has found its way into Christian lectionaries, partly because the situations, culture, and world-view differ so drastically from today's world. Opponents of homosexual rights have recently begun to select and preach on verses from among this material, as have persons supporting capital punishment. Advocates or opponents of various causes have historically justified their positions by referring to this body of material. The witch hunters in colonial New England and the slaveowners in the early nineteenth century, for example, justified their positions by quoting the Old Testament law.

What of the law in the New Testament? The presence of the law pervades its pages. Jesus and his followers were steeped in it. Around the observance of the law swirled most of its controversies. But it was the most law-abiding group, the Pharisees, that conspired with the Romans to send Jesus to his death. What this fact suggests is that the observance of the law may conceal, rather than reveal the human situation. Its provoking of controversy—particularly at Galatia—suggests a second misuse of the law in the New Testament: it is easily distorted to becoming a means of earning God's favor.

Two pitfalls await the biblical preacher in dealing with legal passages. One is identifying the law with the nature and activity of God; the other is using it to define the response God calls for. The preacher who places God the law-giver or his laws at the theological center of the sermon misunderstands the Christian faith. The point of Christ's death and resurrection is that on the cross he satisfied the demands of the law. Paul put the argument insightfully and elegantly in Romans 8:2. "For the law of the Spirit of life in Christ Jesus has set me free from the law of sin and death." If, on the other hand, the law creeps into the response section of the hermeneutical process, the sermon is almost sure to become moralistic.

The intent of the law in Christian theology is to awaken us to our distance from the will and purpose of God; it is not to provide us with ethical instruction. The Ten Commandments do not primarily teach us how to live; they document the depth of our guilt before God—the alienation we have brought upon ourselves. The one commandment that is ours to obey is in Jesus' words. "A new commandment I give to you, that you love one another" (John 13:34).

PROPHECY

Prophecy is the fourth major category of biblical literature. From Mosaic times to the opening days of the New Testament, the prophets spoke the word of God for their time. In groups or individually they traveled throughout Israel to instruct the people and to revive faith in Yahweh. By their words and their holy lives they fought injustice and paganism, advised and excoriated kings, gained and used political power, and predicted the outcome of national events.

Prophetic materials are grossly underutilized in Christian

preaching. The beauty and depth of the prophets' insights into the human situation is an endless resource for texts and for illustrative material. So also is their understanding of God and their grasp of the ethical outworking of the gospel that we have labelled response.

WISDOM

Wisdom literature, the fifth literary genre, is of three basic types: (1) the *mashal*, the short, polished aphorisms that comprise most of The Proverbs or the extended address of the same kind, such as appears in the first nine chapters of Proverbs or Job 28; (2) the riddles and fables that dot the Old Testament; and (3) the sayings of Jesus.

Preaching on wisdom literature has never been popular in the Christian church; most of it is both unread and unfamiliar. The reason is that it seems to have no place in the revelation of God. It does not deal with the mighty acts of God, election faith, covenant faith, or the cultic acts of worship. Much of it can be called secular, humanistic, or utilitarian. For purposes of preaching, however, it contains much that illumines the human situation. The book of Ecclesiastes offers a strong statement of the limits of human ability to perceive the meaning of life. In its famous passage on time in 3:1-9, however, a forceful theological statement is made; if understood in the context of 3:11*a*, "He has made everything beautiful in its time; also he has put eternity into man's mind." And in Proverbs 25:6-22 are two passages that the New Testament uses as the response of the person rightly related to God; one on humility (25:6, 7; see Luke 14:7-11) and the other on feeding one's enemy (25:21; see Rom. 12:20).

Whether a wisdom passage is an aphorism—a wise saying (Prov. 15:17)—or takes the form of a riddle (Judg. 14:10-20) or a fable (II Kings 14:8-10) or is a statement by Jesus (Mark 7:15), the preacher decides whether the material basically unfolds human need, reveals God, or calls for response. That decided, the preacher can proceed.

GOSPELS

A unique literary genre in the Bible are the Gospels: Matthew, Mark, and Luke, are three Synoptic Gospels, and the Gospel

According to John. They are popularly thought of as biography but are actually a unique literary form whose interest in the details of Jesus' life as such are quite secondary.

One thing that makes them unique as a literary genre is the purpose: "These are written that you may believe that Jesus is the Christ, the Son of God, and that believing you may have life in his name" (John 20:31). In a sense, the Gospels are extended evangelical tracts. The other part of their uniqueness is the variety of literary forms found within them: narrative of several kinds, poetry, interpretations of the law, prophetic utterance, and wise sayings.

As in each of the other genres, the preacher-interpreter seeks the theological function or functions of each pericope to discover how God may want to use it in a preaching event.

EPISTLES

Epistles are the seventh literary genre in the Bible. They are the most diverse since they also include a number of other forms—narration of events, fragments of hymns, creedal formulas, theological reflections, and highly personal advice, among other things. The larger body of epistles were written by Paul to deal with problems arising in the churches for which he held himself responsible, and to set forth his understanding of the Christian faith. Like each of the other genres, the epistles fulfill the expectation that the Scriptures will tell us who we are apart from God, will reveal God's gracious action among us, and direction for responding to his grace.

To achieve those aims, the epistles perform both theological and ethical functions. The theological dimension of the epistles is the *kerygma*, the basic outline of early Christian preaching: the Old Testament prophecies have been fulfilled and the new age has dawned; the long-awaited Messiah has now come in Jesus of Nazareth, who, by the power of God, did mighty works, died for our sins, was raised from the dead, is now exalted at the right hand of God, and will come again to be the judge of all mankind; therefore, let all who hear repent and be baptized for the forgiveness of their sins.

The ethical dimension of the epistles is included in the *didache*, the teachings appropriate for the instruction of the new converts. These materials explore the area of Christian conduct, especially important for those who entered the Christian community from outside Judaism.

APOCALYPTIC

Apocalyptic writings conclude the list of literary genres of the Bible. Set in the context of political and personal persecution, these writings offer hope to the readers that God has not forsaken them and that he will vindicate them in his own time, bringing justice to pass. No evil men or governments, the apocalyptic books declare, can ultimately thwart the purposes of God.

Daniel and Revelation are the two apocalyptic books in the canonical Bible, joined in the apocryphal books by II Esdras. The authors are not known, but internal evidence makes the dating quite exact. The apocalyptic style is visionary, fanciful, and symbolic; to have clearly written material in hand would have meant certain death for persons found in possession of the document. Daniel, therefore, writes, not of the ruler Antiochus Epiphanes, but of a "little horn" (8:9) and a "king of the north" (11:40). The author of Revelation symbolizes Rome as a great harlot seated on many waters and drunk with the blood of the saints and martyrs of Jesus (17:1-6).

For the contemporary biblical preacher, the apocalyptic writings are a challenging and exciting resource. Through the popular press, many church members have been faced for the first time with interpretations of these books that are not in the mainstream of traditional Christian belief and responsible biblical scholarship. Like ancient Israel and the New Testament church under Roman persecution, today's society is subject to tremendous emotional stress, uncertain of its future, and cognizant as never before of the deep and apparently hopeless corruption of human nature and human governments. It awaits a word from Christian pulpits that God in Christ is alive in this kind of world too and is calling its people to respond to his gracious, transforming love.

Whatever the literary genre, the Bible continues to communicate the gracious love of God to those who search its pages. When that searching is done with exegetical skill and hermeneutical insight, biblical preaching becomes possible. And how beautiful and powerful is that preaching that enables listeners to respond to God's word by loving the world with God's love!

NOTES

CHAPTER I

1. Donald G. Miller, *The Way to Biblical Preaching* (Nashville: Abingdon, 1957), p. 26.
2. Leander Keck, *The Bible in the Pulpit* (Nashville: Abingdon, 1978), p. 106.
3. Lloyd M. Perry, *Biblical Preaching for Today's World* (Chicago: Moody Press, 1973), p. 78, 79.
4. See James Smart, *The Strange Silence of the Bible in the Churches* (Philadelphia: The Westminster Press, 1970) for a keen analysis of this hiatus.

CHAPTER II

1. James A. Sanders in "Hermeneutics," in *The Interpreter's Dictionary of the Bible: Supplementary Volume* (Nashville: Abingdon, 1976), p. 403.
2. James D. Smart. *The Past, Present, and Future of Biblical Theology* (Philadelphia: The Westminster Press, 1979), p. 43.
3. *Ibid.*, p. 43.
4. Leander E. Keck and Gene M. Tucker, "Exegesis" in *The Interpreter's Dictionary of the Bible: Supplementary Volume* (Nashville: Abingdon, 1976), p. 298.
5. Published by the Consultation on Church Union, 228 Alexander Street, Princeton, NJ 08540.
6. An excellent example is in her *Creative Preaching* (Nashville: Abingdon, 1980) pp. 64, 65. Also see her *Old Testament and the Proclamation of the Gospel* (Philadelphia: The Westminster Press, 1973), p. 142.
7. See James Earl Massey's *Designing the Sermon* (Nashville: Abingdon, 1980) for some examples.
8. A simple, understandable introduction to this discipline is John Reumann's article, "The Transmisson of the Biblical Text" in *The Interpreter's One-Volume Commentary on the Bible* (Nashville: Abingdon, 1971), pp. 1225-36.
9. Bruce M. Metzger, *A Textual Commentary on the Greek New Testament* (London-New York: United Bible Societies, 1971).
10. Justo and Catherine Gonzalez, *Liberation Preaching* (Nashville: Abingdon, 1980), p. 35.
11. Walter Wink, *The Bible in Human Transformation* (Philadelphia: Fortress Press, 1973), p. 1.
12. James L. Mays, "Editorial," *Interpretation* (April, 1980), p. 182.
13. David J. A. Clines, "Story and Poem: The Old Testament as Literature and as Scripture," *Interpretation* (April, 1980), p. 118.
14. Smart, *Past, Present, and Future,* p. 128.
15. Gerhard Lohfink, *The Bible: Now I Get It!* (Garden City: Doubleday, 1979), p. 33.

16. Raymond Brown, "Canonicity," *The Jerome Biblical Commentary* (Englewood Cliffs: Prentice-Hall, 1968), II, pp. 531-32.
17. Keck and Tucker, "Exegesis," p. 302.
18. Gabriel Fackre, *The Christian Story*, (Grand Rapids: Eerdmans, 1978).
19. Victor Paul Furnish, "Some Practical Guidelines for New Testament Exegesis," *Perkins Journal* (Spring, 1973) pp. 1-16.
20. Brevard Childs, *The Book of Exodus* (Philadelphia: The Westminster Press, 1974); *Introduction to the Old Testament as Scripture* (Philadelphia: Fortress Press 1979).
21. Titles of reference books in print for the categories discussed in this section are listed in the appendix.

CHAPTER III

1. Wink, *The Bible in Human Transformation*, p. 2.
2. Rudolph Bultmann, *Existence and Faith* (London: Hodder & Stoughton, 1961), pp. 343-44.
3. Wolfhart Pannenberg, *Revelation as History* (New York: The Macmillan Company, 1968).
4. Jurgen Moltmann, *Theology of Hope* (New York: Harper & Row, 1967.) pp. 106-12.
5. Leander Keck, *The Bible in the Pulpit* (Nashville: Abingdon, 1978), p. 117.
6. Ernst Fuchs, "The New Testament and the Hermeneutical Problem," in *The New Hermeneutic*, Volume II of *New Frontiers in Theology*. (New York: Harper & Row, 1964).
7. Gerhard Kittel, ed. *Theological Dictionary of the New Testament*, Volume III (Grand Rapids, Mich.: Eerdmans Publishing Co., 1965), p. 573.
8. John Calvin, *Commentaries on the Epistles of Paul to the Galatians and Ephesians* (Edinburgh: Calvin Translation Society, 1854), p. 136.
9. Ronald A. Knox, "The Window in the Wall," in *The Twentieth-Century Pulpit* ed. James W. Cox (Nashville: Abingdon, 1978), p. 125.
10. James M. Robinson, "Hermeneutics Since Barth," in *The New Hermeneutic*, Volume II of New Frontiers in Theology (New York: Harper & Row, 1964), pp. 23-24.
11. Elizabeth Achtemeier, *Creative Preaching*, p. 66.
12. Keck, *Bible in the Pulpit*, pp. 115-16.
13. Ernest Best, *From Text to Sermon* (Atlanta: John Knox, 1978), chapters 1-2.
14. Gonzalez and Gonzalez, *Liberation Preaching*, p. 16.
15. James A. Sanders, *God Has a Story Too*. (Philadelphia: Fortress Press, 1979) p. 5.
16. Lohfink, *Now I Get It!*, p. 43.
17. Gordon Fee, *Interpreting the Word of God*, ed. Samuel Schultz and Morris Inch (Chicago: Moody Press, 1976), pp. 105-6.
See also Charles H. Kraft, *Christianity in Culture* (Maryknoll, NY: Orbis Books, 1979) for an extensive investigation of this theme.
18. Robert Tannehill, "Tension in Synoptic Sayings and Stories," in *Interpretation* (April, 1980), pp. 144-47.
19. Gerhard Ebeling, *The Nature of Faith* (Philadelphia: Fortress Press, 1968, pp. 87, 183.
20. Gerhard Ebeling, *Word and Faith* (Philadelphia: Fortress Press, 1963), p. 318.

21. See Berkeley Mickelson, *Intrpreting the Bible* (Grand Rapids: Eerdmans, 1963) for additional material on figures of speech in chapters 8–10; also chapters 11–12 for data on typology and symbols.
22. Sanders, *God Has a Story Too*, p. 134.
23. See Edmund A. Steimle, Morris J. Niedenthal, and Charles L. Rice, *Preaching the Story*. (Philadelphia: Fortress Press, 1980) for an excellent resource in this area.
24. Sanders, *God Has a Story Too*, p. 20.
25. Gonzalez and Gonzalez, *Liberation Preaching*, p. 101.
26. James A. Sanders, "Hermeneutics," p. 407.
27. Kraft, *Christianity in Culture.* p. 9.
28. Sanders, *God Has a Story Too*, p. 15.

CHAPTER IV

1. Paul Tillich, *Systematic Theology, Volume I* (Chicago: University of Chicago Press, 1951), p. 62.
2. Harry Emerson Fosdick, *The Living of These Days* (New York: Harper & Brothers, 1956), p. 94.
3. John Dewey, *How We Think* (Boston: D. C. Heath & Co., 1933), chap. 7.
4. Milton Crum, *Manual on Preaching* (Valley Forge: Judson Press, 1977), p. 20.
5. Gary Cronkhite, *Persuasion: Speech and Behavioral Change* (New York: Bobbs-Merrill, 1969), pp. 193, 197.
6. Herman Stuempfle, *Preaching Law and Gospel* (Philadelphia: Fortress Press 1978).
7. Heinrich Ott, *Theology and Preaching* (Philadelphia: The Westminster Press, 1965) p. 53.
8. Crum, *Manual on Preaching*, pp. 20-21.

FOR FURTHER READING

CHAPTER I: THE CHALLENGE OF BIBLICAL PREACHING

Abbey, Merrill R. *Communication in Pulpit and Parish*. Philadelphia: The Westminster Press, 1973.
Browne, R. E. C. *The Ministry of the Word*. Philadelphia: Fortress Press, 1976.
Buechner, Frederick. *Telling the Truth*. San Francisco; Harper & Row, 1977.
Craddock, Fred B. *Overhearing the Gospel*. Nashville: Abingdon, 1978.
Fant, Clyde. *Preaching for Today*. New York: Harper & Row, 1975.
Mitchell, Henry H. *The Recovery of Preaching*. San Francisco: Harper & Row, 1977.

CHAPTER II: THE TASK OF EXEGESIS

Kaiser, Otto and Kümmel, W. G., *Exegetical Method*. New York: Seabury Press, 1963.
Krentz, Edgar. *The Historical-Critical Method*. Philadelphia: Fortress Press, 1975.
Longenecker, Richard. *Biblical Exegesis in the Apostolic Period*. Grand Rapids: Eerdmans Publishing Co., 1975.
Scholer, David M. *A Basic Bibliographic Guide for New Testament Exegesis*. Grand Rapids: Eerdmans, 1975.
Soulen, Richard. *Handbook of Biblical Criticism*. Atlanta: John Knox Press, 1976.
Stuart, Douglas. *Old Testament Exegesis: A Primer for Students and Pastors*. Philadelphia: The Westminster Press, 1980.

CHAPTER III: THE PROCESS OF INTERPRETATION

Harrington, Daniel J. *Interpreting the New Testament*. Wilmington, DE: Michael Glazier, 1979.
Marshall, I. Howard (ed.). *New Testament Interpretation: Essays on Principles and Methods*. Grand Rapids: Eerdmans, 1977.
Mickelsen, A. Berkeley. *Interpreting the Bible*. Grand Rapids: Eerdmans, 1963.
Ramm, Bernard. *Protestant Biblical Interpretation* (Third Revised Edition) Grand Rapids: Baker Book House., 1970.
Rogers, Jack B. and Donald M. McKim. *The Authority and Interpretation of the Bible*. San Franscisco: Harper & Row, 1979.

CHAPTER IV: A METHODOLOGY FOR BIBLICAL PREACHING

Crum, Milton. *Manual on Preaching*. Valley Forge: Judson Press, 1977.
Lowry, Eugene L. *The Homiletical Plot*. Atlanta: John Knox Press, 1980.

Massey, James Earl. *Designing the Sermon: Order and Movement in Preaching.* Nashville: Abingdon, 1980.

CHAPTER V: A CASE STUDY

Edwards, O. C., Jr. *The Living and Active Word.* New York: Seabury Press, 1975.
McCurley, Foster, R., Jr. *Proclaiming the Promise: Christian Preaching from the Old Testament.* Philadelphia: Fortress Press, 1974.
von Rad, Gerhard. *Biblical Interpretations in Preaching.* Nashville: Abingdon, 1977.

CHAPTER VI: GUIDELINES FOR PREACHING BIBLICAL GENRES

Gowan, Donald E. *Reclaiming the Old Testament for the Christian Pulpit.* Atlanta: John Knox Press, 1980.
Smith, D. Moody. *Interpreting the Gospels for Preaching.* Philadelphia: Fortress Press, 1980.

APPENDIX
EXEGETICAL TOOLS

CONCORDANCES

Nelson's Complete Concordance of the Revised Standard Version of the Bible. New York: Thomas Nelson & Sons, 1957.

Strong, James. *The Exhaustive Concordance of the Bible.* Nashville: Abingdon, 1961.

Young, Robert. *Analytical Concordance to the Bible,* 22nd edition. Grand Rapids: Eerdmans, 1955.

WORD STUDIES

Botterweek, G. Johannes and H. Ringgren (eds.). *Theological Dictionary of the Old Testament.* Grand Rapids: Eerdmans, 1974.

Brown, Colin (ed.). *The New International Dictionary of New Testament Theology.* Grand Rapids: Zondervan, 1975-78.

Kittel, Gerhard and Gerhard Friedrich (eds.). *Theological Dictionary of the New Testament* (translated by G. W. Bromiley). Grand Rapids: Eerdmans, 1964-76.

Richardson, Alan. *A Theological Word Book of the Bible.* New York: Macmillan, 1950.

COMMENTARIES

Barclay, William. *Daily Study Bible.* Philadelphia: Westminster Press, 1975-76.

Buttrick, George A. (ed.). *The Interpreter's Bible.* Nashville: Abingdon, 1957.

Freedman, David Noel, et. al. (eds.). *The Anchor Bible.* New York: Doubleday, 1964.

Hanson, Paul D., et. al. (eds.). *Hermeneia* (6 volumes). Philadelphia: Fortress Press, 1971-76.

Laymon, Charles M. *The Interpreter's One-Volume Commentary on the Bible.* Nashville: Abingdon, 1971.

DICTIONARIES AND ENCYCLOPEDIAS

Bromiley, Geoffrey W. (ed.). *The International Standard Bible Encyclopedia, Rev. Ed.,* 4 volumes. Grand Rapids: Eerdmans, 1979.

Buttrick, George Arthur and Keith Crim (eds.). *The Interpreter's Dictionary of the Bible: An Illustrated Encyclopedia,* 5 volumes. Nashville: Abingdon, 1962-1976.

ATLASES

Aharoni, Jochanan. *The Macmillan Bible Atlas.* New York: Macmillan, 1968.

May, Herbert Gordon. *Oxford Bible Atlas.* New York: Oxford University Press, 1974.

GUIDES TO BIBLICAL STUDY

Aland, Kurt (ed.). *Synopsis of the Four Gospels*. Stuttgart: United Bible Societies, 1964.

Blair, Edward P. *Abingdon Bible Handbook*. Nashville: Abingdon, 1975.

Childs, Brevard S. *Old Testament Books for Pastor and Teacher*. Philadelphia: Westminster, 1977.

Danker, Frederick W. *Multipurpose Tools for Bible Study*, 3rd edition. St. Louis: Concordia, 1970.

Francis, Fred O. and J. Paul Sampley (eds.). *Pauline Parallels*. Philadelphia: Fortress Press, 1975.

Joy, Charles R. (ed.). *Harper's Topical Concordance*. New York: Harper & Brothers, 1961.

Scholer, David M. *A Basic Bibliographic Guide to New Testament Exegesis*, 2nd ed. Grand Rapids: Eerdmans, 1973.

Viening, Edward (ed.). *The Zondervan Topical Bible*. Grand Rapids: Zondervan, 1969.

ORIGINAL LANGUAGE SOURCES

Lexicons

Bauer, Walter; William F. Arndt; and F. Wilbur Gingrich. *A Greek-English Lexicon of the New Testament and Other Early Christian Literature*, 2nd ed. Chicago: University of Chicago Press, 1979.

Gesenius, William; Francis Brown; S. R. Driver; and Charles A. Briggs. *A Hebrew and English Lexicon of the Old Testament*. Oxford: Clarendon Press, 1952.

Concordance for Greek New Testament

Moulton, W. F. and A. S. Geden. *A Concordance of the Greek Testament According to the Tests of Westcott and Hort, Tischendorf and the English Revisers*, 5th ed. Edinburgh: T. & T. Clark, 1978.

Grammars

Blass, F. W., A. Debrunner, and R. W. Funk. *A Greek Grammar of the New Testament*. Chicago: University of Chicago Press, 1961.

Gesenius, William, E. Kautzsch and A. E. Cowley. *Hebrew Grammar*, 2nd ed. Oxford: Clarendon, 1910.

INDEX OF BIBLICAL REFERENCES